Shadow

of

Defeat

by

Elfi Hornby

ISBN: 0-9741062-0-8

Library of Congress Control Number:
2003105487

Cover:
Artist Sketch - Elfi Hornby
Graphic Adaptation - Corkey Hollaway

Printed in the United States of America by
Maverick Publications, Inc. • Bend, Oregon

Acknowledgments

*My heart is overflowing with gratitude for the generosity,
help and support from family and friends.*

Very special thanks to...

...my dear husband Jim and son Robert for their loving support and understanding; for granting me the space and time to complete this project.

...my enthusiastic and untiring promoter and friend Kelly Creso and his wife Mary Jo for getting my message out.

...my neighbor and friend Corkey Hollaway for his creative graphics, and the many hours he spent guiding me through computer problems.

...my mentor, teacher, editor, and friend, Joan Tornow, who keeps me inspired.

...my writer friends for their encouragement.

...my first readers and friends: Val Dumond, Jack and Francine Aylward, Robert and Stephanie Reynolds, Joyce Elijah, Hildegard von Waldenburg for their input and critique.

...my promoters—family and friends—in Helena Montana

...Gary Asher, Maverick Publications, for his extra-special, personal assistance in producing this book.

Introduction

As a young dancer with the *Molkow Ballett*, a small ballet company from Berlin, I spent six harrowing months on the Russian front at the height of WW II, in 1943, entertaining German troops. Facing incredible hardships and challenges, being exposed to all the horrors of war, I miraculously survived. I was seventeen. Even then, I knew that I had to write about this some day, and I did, in my first book, *Dancing to War*.

The last year and months of war and its aftermath were even more horrendous. When illness forced me in the spring of 1944 to leave the ballet company and return home, I was ready. My parents were relieved. I would have rather perished with them than living in continuous agony, not knowing if they had survived the latest bombings raids. I was nineteen when the war ended and a nervous wreck. The aftermath was no less traumatic. Again, I felt compelled to write about this period. For my fellow Americans, and for the sake of history, I want to describe what life was like in Germany before, during, and after the war. Much is written about this time in history, mostly from a point of looking from the outside in, and is often fraught with misconceptions, assumptions, prejudice, and ignorance. One has to walk the walk to understand. Thus, I invite the reader to walk with me through this tumultuous period in history.

Contents

Mitzi (Elfi) as La Argentina.

Chapter 1

From Conqueror to Conquered

As World War II ground to its tragic, bloody end in Europe, disintegrating German forces fought their last desperate battles to stem the Russian tide, but offered only sporadic resistance against the lesser-feared Western forces. By late April 1945, the American army had reached the outskirts of my hometown—Munich, Germany. Hundreds of thousands of citizens still living among the city's bombed-out, burned-out ruins feared and prepared for the worst. Munich's defiant *Gauleiter*, area commander of the collapsing Nazi government, continued to broadcast from his bombproof bunker, ordering every man, woman and child to defend the city by whatever means possible. The Allies, on the other hand, demanded unconditional surrender or threatened to bomb what was left of Munich into the ground. People held their breaths. A few hard-core fanatics, not yet ready to give up, could cause a last minute slaughter.

1

I was nineteen. Like most people, I was sick of the war, sick of being hungry, sick of scrounging around for the barest necessities, sick of ducking day and night into crowded air raid shelters, trembling, praying, wondering if the next bomb was meant for me. My life, my dreams, my career—I was a classical dancer—my future, all lay in shambles. My brother was dead. So were many of my closest friends. At times, I truly envied them. Then again, I wanted to live, to live a life I could only imagine, a life free of fear and beyond mere survival.

When I looked in the mirror, I despaired. Staring back at me was a face drained of life and youth, pale and gaunt, with eyes dulled by the horrors they had seen. Not even makeup could brighten my appearance. My hair, washed with homemade laundry soap, hung in dark, oily, lusterless strands down over my shoulders. My clothes were faded, frayed, ill-fitting hand-me-downs I tried to dress up with a necklace or broach. But inside me beat the heart of a young woman who, like a butterfly waiting to break out of its cocoon, wondered if the day would ever come when she could spread her wings.

I shared my parents' three-room apartment at the outskirts of Munich, in a nice, newer development with broad streets, flagstone sidewalks and large areas of green space. We had been lucky, oh, so lucky that our unit was one of few that had escaped major bomb damage. Some of the other block-long, two and three story apartment buildings had sustained direct hits. Diagonally across the street from us, an air-mine had blasted away an entire street corner, killing all who had sought safety in the cellar. The end of our block had burned to the ground during a rain of incendiary bombs that had caused a horrifying, blazing, citywide inferno. Sheer luck and the heroic acts by residents, who risked their lives to douse the fires, had saved the units in between.

During one such air raid, my father and a neighbor—both air raid wardens—were patrolling our building when two stick-bombs crashed through the roof. Without giving it a second thought, the men grabbed and tossed them out the window before they could explode. Their quick action did save our home, but it could have cost them their lives. Every time we emerged from the air raid shelter and found all four walls of our apartment intact, we considered it a miracle.

Our luck held even through one of the last, most terrifying day-raids. Already before the first sirens wailed, we could hear the distant drone of approaching bombers. Hundreds, maybe thousands of them soon darkened the sky, causing windows, walls and the ground to vibrate even before the first bombs whistled to the ground and exploded.

"This is going to be a big one," my father warned and hustled everybody down into the shelter. We had barely closed its iron door when bombs screamed down around us, exploding, sucking the air out of our lungs. I saw the cement floor heave and the mortar crack and fall off the walls. Choking dust filled the air. Having survived the first wave of bombers, we listened in frozen panic for the next. As if someone had held a loaded gun to our heads, death seemed only a click away. Not even being at the front lines in Russia was as unnerving. I could no longer hide my terror. With the first sound of the sirens, all strength drained from my body. My legs buckled under me, and my hands shook so hard that I could not hold a spoon or cup without spilling its contents.

That particular day, we thought the end had come for sure. The attack had lasted what seemed like an eternity. When it was finally over and the 'all clear' sounded, we were afraid to move, afraid to come up, afraid of what we would find. Amazingly, our building had survived again. However, within just a hundred-yard radius, we counted sixteen craters with unexploded bombs in them. Any one of them could still wipe us out. Fortunately, they were duds, not time bombs. After several nerve-racking days, a bomb squad made up of volunteers from prisons and concentration camps, whose dangerous work earned them extra food and privileges, finally disarmed and removed them. Once more, we had survived. Now we faced the uncertainty of occupation. Would there be fighting in the streets? What would it be like to meet our enemy face to face?

We did not have to wait long to find out. Word spread that American tanks were seen rolling through the heart of Munich, about to bridge the Isar River, heading in our direction. Not knowing what to expect, my mother, a gray-haired, frail but feisty little woman in her late fifties, hurriedly gathered clothing, bedding and what little food we had to take to the cellar. My father and I filled buckets and pans with water for drinking and for fighting fires. Our neighbors did the same.

Next door to us lived Herr and Frau Kloh with their widowed daughter and little grandson. Old Kloh had a bad case of asthma. His wife, thin as a rail, kept house and took care of three-year-old Rolfi, whose mother worked as a bookkeeper somewhere. Above us lived a childless couple, a short, bald-headed, pedantic bureaucrat and his forever cleaning, scrubbing wife. Across the hall from them lived the Koenigs. We saw or knew very little of them. Herr Koenig had recently come home on leave and his wife worked in a factory.

4

Up and down our street, improvised white flags appeared outside windows. My father and Herr Kloh had just decided to hang one out, also, when Herr Koenig, in uniform, rifle in hand, came down the stairs. Highly agitated, he commanded my father and Herr Kloh to barricade front and back doors and arm themselves with whatever they had. We stared at him in utter disbelief.

"Are you crazy?" Old Kloh said to him. "You want us all to get killed? The war is over. It's over! Get rid of that rifle, for God's sake."

For days, people had been burning Nazi uniforms and flags, Hitler pictures and books and other Nazi memorabilia in enormous bonfires on city streets. Not Herr Koenig. A Nazi to the end, he boldly wore a swastika armband.

"Do your duty or else," he ordered, pointing the gun barrel at the men.

My heart stopped. Then, as if on cue, Frau Kloh, her daughter, my mother and I rushed the crazed man, took his gun away and ripped the armband off his sleeve. My father, a tall, lean, quiet man, grabbed him by the lapels and shook him, chewing on words that would not come out of his mouth. When he let go, Herr Koenig backed up the stairs with an expression of contempt.

"I should have turned you in a long time ago," he muttered through clenched teeth. The Klohs got rid of the rifle and armband, but we still worried what Herr Koenig might do next.

Meanwhile, frantic mothers called their children home. Others ripped their still wet laundry off the clotheslines to take in the house. Windows banged shut. Roller shutters creaked down. Finally, a tense, dead quiet settled over the neighborhood as everybody waited, worried and kept secret watch.

For the longest time, nothing happened. Cautiously, first one, then another, people emerged from their cellars. A sunny spring day drew them outside where lilac hedges stood in full bloom, and uncut lawns sparkled with yellow and white flowers. Mother and I joined a group of neighbors in the back yard, venting our anxiety.

Weary of the war, relieved to see it end, yet fearing what might follow, people's feelings vacillated between panic and hope. We had heard rumors that once the fighting had stopped, the Amis—as we called the Americans—acted quite charitably in comparison to the Russians who raped and killed, plundered and burned at random. This gave us hope. Yet, this same enemy had bombed our cities to ashes and dust; indiscriminately killed and incinerated a helpless population by the hundreds of thousands—woman and children, the old and the sick—and destroyed millenniums of irreplaceable art and history. What could we expect? What would happen to us now?

Suddenly our butcher's thirteen year old son raced up on his bike, hair caked to his sweaty forehead, cheeks flushed and eyes gleaming wide. "I saw them! I saw them," he blurted out with what breath he had left. "They are coming up the *Giesinger Berg*," a long hill winding up from the river's valley. "I saw them, sitting atop their tanks. You won't believe this. People by the hundreds line the streets, waving white handkerchiefs. And what do the Amis do? They wave back, smiling, throwing candy, chocolate and cigarettes into the crowd." He pulled a wrapped, half-eaten candy bar out of his pant pocket. "See, I got some, too."

We listened open-mouthed. It sounded incredible. This, I had to see for myself. Against my mother's fearful protests, my father and I hauled our bikes up from the basement and the two of us took off with the butcher's son in the lead. "You'll get yourself killed," my terrified mother cried after us.

Casting all fears to the wind, hearts pounding with hopeful excitement, we pedaled along deserted, rubble-strewn streets, past abandoned streetcars, buses, and the ghostly facades of bombed-out ruins. Then we heard the drone of engines, growing louder, growing into a roar. We turned a corner and saw a wall of people, cheering and waving. Closing in, we saw a column of tanks laboring slowly up the hill with American soldiers sitting on top, just as the boy had told us, waving back, smiling, tossing treats to the crowd that scrambled to catch them. My father caught a partially empty pack of cigarettes and lit one on the spot, handling and savoring it like an expensive cigar. For a good fifteen minutes we stood amidst the cheering crowd watching as if watching a holiday parade. Not a shot was fired. The procession of smiling faces on their deadly mounts seemed endless. I wanted to stay, but fearing that my mother would worry herself sick, my father urged us to return home.

We pedaled back along the same deserted streets, then took a shortcut across a field dotted with craters and strewn with live, unexploded bombs. I dared not to look right or left, lest panic would keep me from going on. I just focused on getting across as quickly as possible.

As we turned into the alley to our apartments, my mother stood waiting by the back door, hands pressed against her heart. She sobbed when she saw us coming. Before we could tell her about the friendly Americans, she informed us that the Amis had seized the airwaves and had ordered all citizens of Munich to remain indoors. Anyone seen on the streets would be arrested or shot.

During the first two days of occupation, our neighborhood saw no sign of the Amis. Despite continued warnings of dire consequences, people sneaked out, doing what they had to. Many had no food, no water, no heat, and no electricity. Others were desperate to check on family, friends and the sick. Mail and telephone service no longer existed. The government with its infrastructure had collapsed. People were left to their own devices.

Finally, less than a mile from our house, Ami troops moved in and took over a large, deserted Nazi warehouse, the *Reichszeugmeisterei*. A few days later they disappeared again, leaving the gates to the complex wide open. Looting started. In broad daylight, ignoring all caution, hoards of people stampeded the building, trampling on and over one another in search of food. Some emerged with buckets full of rice or lentils, sacks of flour, and canned goods; others walked off with bolts of fabric, furniture, rugs, anything they could find. What they could not eat, they could trade on the black market for a can of milk, a slab of bacon, a chunk of butter, cheese, or whatever. Appalled at first, my father and I finally joined the frenzied mob.

Like a trail of ants, people streamed through a labyrinth of hallways and down the stairs to the cellar where they expected the food to be stored. At the entrance to a narrow passage, they elbowed, punched and trampled each other to the ground to get to the food. It was an ugly scene. My father and I turned away, not yet desperate enough.

As we explored other parts of the building, the already ransacked offices and meeting rooms, we discovered a large storage closet. In it we found several rolled-up carpets and odds and ends of furniture, including a leather chair. All this was government property of a government that was no more, a government my father despised.

Ignoring any qualms of conscience he might have had, Papa draped a roll of carpet over my shoulder and hoisted the leather chair upon his. "That's good for a couple of pounds of bacon, and maybe a sack of coal," he estimated.

By the time we reached the street outside the complex, the load proved too heavy to carry all the way home. So, Papa decided I should wait there with the goods while he ran home to get a small handcart. Guarding our loot, I caught sneers from a few passers-by. "Hypocrites!" I muttered, knowing damned well that they would be in there looting with the rest of us, if they did not have some other illegal source to help fill their bellies. For us, it was a matter of survival. I clenched my teeth, stayed and endured, knowing that the chair and rug could be traded for enough food and fuel to tide us over for several weeks. Our needs were desperate.

My mother said nothing when we arrived with our booty. She looked at it joylessly. We laid the rug over the hardwood floor in my room. Papa temporarily claimed the leather chair, replacing his hard, wooden one. When he sat in it for the first time, sinking into its luxurious softness, he acted like a pauper trying out a king's throne. His hands glided admiringly over the smooth leather, and from the expression on his face, I knew what he was thinking. The chair represented status and success, something that had eluded him for most of his life. A cruel childhood, poor health, and strong and unpopular political leanings—he was a stubborn pacifist—kept him poor and from reaching his potential.

Seeing him sit there, wallowing in 'what he could have been', racked my heart with sadness and anger.

While he had no control over his upbringing or his health, I often had questioned his political decisions. Why could he not, like millions of other Germans, have joined the party, paid his dues, and thus been eligible for a decent job to lift his family out of poverty? Most of our friends shared his political convictions, but they played by the rules of the day and prospered. Some worked for changes within the system, which enabled them to do much good. In fact, thanks to them, my father had not landed in a concentration camp. His stubborn political stand had led to many heated discussions between him and me. A chair, a stolen leather chair, I thought bitterly, is all he had to show for his principles.

Among the shabby furniture in our small combination kitchen-living room the chair looked pompously grotesque.

Later, out of sheer curiosity, I went back to the complex and roamed through the spacious, empty offices of our now defunct officialdom. All that was left were large paintings of the *Fuehrer*, some vandalized, plus an enormous flag that covered an entire wall of one of the large, ravaged meeting rooms. I stared at it, estimating how many yards of fabric it must have taken to make it, when a thought flashed through my head. "What a terrific costume this would make! Fire red, perfect for the stage." I could picture it. I saw the upper part straight and fitted to my body, then flair out from mid-hip into a full, ruffled skirt. The black swastika could be used for the trim around the ruffles. On impulse, making sure no one saw me, I ripped the flag off its hangers, bunched it up and under my coat and walked home. I must have looked like twelve-months pregnant with an elephant.

My mother froze when I showed it to her. Long seconds passed before she found her voice. "Have you lost your mind?" she screamed. "Get rid of that...that... Get it out of this house!"

"But Mama...! Just think what a splendid costume this flag would make for a Spanish number," I argued. "Maybe I can dance again...maybe for the Amis."

I had been soloist with the *Molkow Ballett*, a small dance company from Berlin, traveling with it all over Germany and its occupied territories until 1944, when I had to quit because of illness. My costumes, ballet shoes, everything had been supplied by the company. I left with nothing. However, while traveling through German-occupied countries, I noticed that Russian, Polish, and French artists who performed for Germans, were treated and surviving better than most other folk, and thought that I could do that when the day came that the tables turned. That day was here.

"You might as well put a loaded gun to our heads," my mother ranted on, wringing her hands.

"Don't you see that if I am ever to perform again, I will need costumes. You do want me to dance again, don't you?"

"Somebody who finds this in our home may think that we were some Nazi big-shots and arrest us, or shoot us on the spot," Mama worried.

My father, more amused than angry, only shook his head and chuckled. "All these years we never owned a Hitler flag, not even a little one. Now you bring home the biggest one ever made."

Looting took place all over the city. The Amis did not interfere. We heard of people wheeling home cheeses as large as truck tires. Others carried buckets full of wine from cellars flooded with it and where people actually drowned in it. Farmers, on the other hand, had no way to bring their goods to market. They drowned in milk. On foot and on bicycle, city folk— my father and I included—trekked twenty, thirty kilo-

11

meters through woods to the nearest farm for a pitcher of milk, a couple of eggs, or a bag of potatoes. At this point, farmers were glad to get rid of food that would spoil otherwise.

For several days, we saw little to nothing of the Americans. Suddenly, Amis reoccupied the warehouse and then seized many of the surrounding and still undamaged apartment units to house their troops. Residents had only minutes to pack a few personal items before being set on the street with no place to go. They had survived the bombings; now they had lost their home and belongings another way—a tragedy that had everyone in our block trembling. "Will we be next?" My family would not have known where to find shelter.

Before its collapse, the Nazi government had already crowded hundreds of thousands of bombing victims and refugees into every extra square inch of living space. Now, without anybody in charge, what would people do? They had to rely on the pity of weary friends and neighbors, move into tunnels, under ruins, or into makeshift shanties. They had to beg for a spoon to eat with and for rags to sleep on.

The American occupational forces now took control, enforcing a strict curfew. Intermittent broadcasts from the Ami headquarters informed us what we could and could not do. All other news was being passed by word of mouth. Ami guards patrolled our streets. One evening, an older neighbor let his dog out before going to bed that night. He stood in the doorway of his apartment unit when an American MP drove by, spotted him, and hauled him away. Another neighbor, a mother seeking help for her very ill child, met the same fate. We could hear her screaming, "Mein Kind...mein Kind."

Indeed, tables had turned. The conquerors had become the conquered.

In Russia, Poland, and France, I had witnessed the demoralizing effect it had on the people of these countries when we Germans imposed laws and curfews. I already then saw the day coming when I would be walking in their shoes. However, I was also encouraged to see that once the guns fell silent, life seemed to return to a peaceful routine, often in friendly cooperation between civilians and individuals of the occupying forces. While this inspired me with hope, I knew all too well that during a war, soldiers, regardless under what flag they serve, are the nuts and bolts of a killing machine, ready to spring into action upon command. As individuals, I saw them risk their lives to rescue civilians from flaming buildings; as soldiers, obeying a command, I saw them torch entire villages with all that was in it. Such is the mentality of war, and that was what frightened me.

I had learned plenty about the insanity of war during the six months I had to spend on the Russian front in 1943, to entertain German troops. It made me fear what the Americans would do if some idiot like Herr Koenig fired his gun and killed some of them. I had no doubt that they would train their big guns on the area of the sniper and wipe it out with everything and everyone in it. Thank God, Herr Koenig and his wife had disappeared in the interim, but I worried how many of his kind still lurked around.

As the numbing terror of relentless bombings during the last months of war slowly relaxed its grip on me, long suppressed thoughts and feelings returned to mind and heart, paining like blood returning to frozen, thawing flesh. Scenes with faces and voices began to haunt me, faces I would never see again, and voices I would never hear again. Many a night I woke up bathed in sweat as some of my most terrifying experiences replayed in my dreams in nightmarish reality. In one such dream, I saw myself standing again amidst the smoldering ruins of the Icho School, gathering body parts of children. I tried feverishly but in vain to reattach them to the bodies of the victims as if patching broken dolls. Another time, I was back in Russia, in the chapel where I had stumbled on to a mound of mutilated bodies stacked in front of the altar. I wanted to run, but could not move. I wanted to scream, but had no voice. The paralyzing fear I had experienced back then, I relived again and again in my dreams. One of the worst nightmares haunting me was a charred, blood-oozing figure staggering toward me, calling for help, "Au secour, camarad, au secour!" He was one of the tragic victims of a train wreck near Lyon, France, where the train I was on collided with the wreckage of another, blown up only hours before by the French Underground to free Italian prisoners. Coaches crammed full with French civilians had stacked up like toys and burst into flames, turning night into day. In my dreams, as in reality, I felt again this torturous, heartbreaking helplessness. I had to watch this pulp of a human being expire before my eyes. "Help! Help! Please! Somebody help!" My yelling woke me up. The shadow of these nightmares hung over the rest of the day and stole the glimmer of any happier moment.

At nineteen, I knew more about death and dying than of life and living.

On a table next to my bed stood a photo of Willi, my stepbrother, an Olympic hopeful. He had walked into my life, tall and proud, when I was already in my teens. I believed that he was heaven-sent; the answer to my most fervent childhood prayers for a brother or sister. Only a few short years of knowing him, death took him away again. He had been killed in the battle of Stalingrad.

14

Next to his photo, against a stack of tear-stained letters, leaned a picture of Pepi, my first true love. His last letter read, "This note leaves with the last plane out. We are trapped. The Russians will either kill us or take us prisoners. Goodbye, my Love. My thoughts are with you to the end."

For the longest time, I had no tears left to cry. What amazed me was that I was still living when I felt so dead inside.

Since a week before the American occupation, I had not seen or heard from any of my friends or co-workers from the factory where I had to work. Feeling caged, bored, and depressed, I sat for hours by the window, watching armed Ami guards pace up and down the street. They looked neither right nor left, and bothered no one. I wondered what went through their minds. What did they think and feel about us, the enemy—an enemy they had fought fiercely only days before? Did they hate us still? My mother, who had spent several years in the United States and spoke English quite well, addressed one of them with a friendly, "How do you do?" but received no response.

Late one night, while Mama and I were darning socks and Papa was listening to the English radio station, the doorbell rang and someone pounded violently on the outer door of our unit, scaring us out of our seats. Mama dropped her darning, and the three of us stood frozen to the spot, afraid to breathe, looking questioningly from one to the other, "What should we do? Should we respond? See who it is? And what they want?" The doorbelling and pounding continued. Male voices shouted, "Open up! Raus...kommen du raus...schnell...we shoot...bang-bang-bang."

"Amis," Papa whispered. He looked through a peephole out into the stairway to see if any of our neighbors had responded. It was dark and quiet.

"What could they want? Unless we do something, they may break down the door or shoot their way in." Turning to my mother he whispered, "Maybe you could talk to them in English and ask what they want and try to reason with them?" Quietly, he opened a window behind closed shutters and my mother called out, "Hello! Are you looking for someone?"

"Open up, or we shoot," the men answered.

"What do you want? It's late. People are in bed."

"We want Nazis...guns."

"We are no Nazis, we have no guns."

"Open up! Schnell...schnell...."

We felt we had no choice but to open the door. They could throw a grenade or start shooting. There was nobody that could or would help us. My father, with my mother breathing down his back, went to the door and unlocked it. Two Ami soldiers, revolvers in hand, pushed him aside and staggered in, reeking of alcohol. They started searching our place. When they saw me, they paused, their eyes scanning me up and down. Mama, with a stern expression on her face, said something in English to them. It sounded like she was scolding them. They seemed surprised.

"Where did you learn to speak English?" they asked her.

"I was in America. Still have two sisters in Philadelphia," she replied.

I never know how she had found the strength to answer. I was scared mute. The Amis, satisfied that our place was secure, tucked their guns away. Their attitude had suddenly changed. Papa pulled out two kitchen chairs and invited them to sit down. They did. One of them, a tall, burly looking fellow with curly, sandy colored hair offered Papa a cigarette.

"Danke," Papa said.

"You don't speak English?"

16

Papa shook his head, "Nix English."

"And you?" They turned to me.

I shook my head. "Very little," I said.

The other fellow, shorter and stockier, with a crew cut and sky blue eyes, reached into his coat pocket, pulled out a bottle and set it on the table. "We need glasses, Mom?" he said. Mama sat two shot glasses in front of them.

"We need three more, one for you, one for Pops, and one for...hey...what's your name?" Blue-eyes looked at me.

"Mitzi," I replied, giving my nickname. "What is yours?" I asked, looking straight into his eyes, not letting on how scared I was.

He hesitated then said, "I'm Bob, that's Harry." It was obvious that they did not give their real names.

They stayed until after one o'clock that night. My mother showed them albums with old photos she had from her time in the United States. Papa sat contently in his leather chair, smoking their cigarettes and drinking their whisky, his mind far off somewhere. I listened intently, recognizing a word here, a phrase there, only to find my school English totally inadequate. Finally they left with a promise to come back.

What their purpose was to pound on our front door that night remained a mystery. I had a hunch that my mother's English had saved us from their original intent. In their inebriated state, who knows what they had in mind.

Disobeying orders not to fraternize with Germans, Bob and Harry visited us frequently from that night on, and always with their pockets bulging. They brought us Spam, sardines and other canned goods, as well as cigarettes for Pops, and coffee...instant coffee...real coffee. And always, they brought a bottle with them.

We never saw them fully sober, nor ever so drunk that they could not handle themselves.

The visits by the Americans with their bulging pockets did not go unnoticed by our neighbors. Gossips sharpened their tongues with vicious speculations, fueled by jealousy, which in turn leaked back to us. Frau Kloh and the bald-headed pedant from above, who had never liked one another before, suddenly spent hours in the stairway talking, only to fall silent the moment one of us appeared. I felt the frost in their voices as we exchanged greetings.

In the days and weeks to come, life gradually took on a new routine. A few remaining stores reopened for short periods each day, provided they had anything to sell. Every morning, long lines formed in front of the neighborhood bakery, hours before it opened. In minutes, the bread was sold out and many, who had waited so long, left empty handed. Even if we were lucky to get a loaf, I could not eat it. It tasted moldy. The baker said that it was made with flour from America. I preferred our own bread made with flour salvaged from a bombed-out mill. The force of explosions had saturated it with grit from pulverized brick and stone. Each bite crunched between the teeth like chewing on sand, but it tasted better.

Slowly, trams and buses began to run again on sporadic schedules. Other traffic consisted mostly of US Army vehicles, a few horse drawn wagons, bicyclists, and pedestrians. Along *Nauplia Strasse*, a main road leading in and out of the city, a steady stream of dead-weary German solders plodded homeward. The Amis no longer seemed to bother taking prisoners. Women with photographs of a missing son or husband besieged the haggard stragglers, "Have you seen him? Have you seen him?" Without breaking their labored pace, the men glanced at the photos, shook their heads sadly, and trudged on. Some compassionate souls set out pitchers with drinking water, a bench or chair for them to rest on, sometimes even a bowl of boiled potatoes, but few stopped, afraid, perhaps, that exhaustion would overtake them and they would not be able to go on. Their only goal now was to get home to their families.

Home? Family? Tragically, many would find only ruins and death.

When they were called to war, they were boys, cocky, self-confident, convinced of their invincibility. Now they seemed old beyond their years. War had dulled their eyes and wiped the smile off their faces. Hollow-cheeked, in tattered uniforms, they personified the meaning of defeat. They were left but shadows of their former selves. My heart ached for them. They were my brothers. During my six months on the Russian front, I had become one of them.

Mitzi (Elfi) 1943.

Parents - 1958

Street where we lived - Immergrünstrasse, Munich

Chapter 2

From the Ashes

Weeks after the first American troops had marched into Munich, the war in Germany officially ended. Hitler was dead, and survivors of the German High Command had signed Germany's surrender. Already months before Germany's final defeat, as Nazi censorship lost its stranglehold, rumors about unimaginable atrocities in Nazi concentration camps began to circulate. What first passed in whispers from ear to ear to dumbstruck listeners now broke into bold headlines. The German nation was made to face its shame.

Most people had known enough about the brutality of the Gestapo and the SS to inspire them with fear. However, most people did not know, and could not even have imagined what went on behind the barbed wires and walls of Nazi prison camps. Almost daily, new revelations, one more outrageously bizarre than the next, stunned the German public into flat denial. It was too much for the average mind to comprehend and accept.

Because of my father's political stand and his open, but passive defiance of the Nazi regime, I suspect that he knew more than most people. For instance, I remember vaguely—I was only about eight years old then—that a former boarder of ours visited my father after being released from Dachau, a concentration camp in the suburbs of Munich. I heard him tell my parents, in a hushed voice, about the cruelty of guards, who flogged prisoners bloody, then sicked vicious dogs on them, looking on and laughing as the men tried to scramble up poles with the dogs tearing at their flesh. He implored my parents never to breathe a word of this to anyone or he would be as good as dead. Merely by listening to, or repeating such accounts, the punishment was just as severe. Still, bits and pieces of such information occasionally did leak out, diminishing into rumors and hearsay since the sources had neither name nor face.

Suddenly, screaming headlines with shocking pictures of concentration camp victims appeared all over town on billboards and *Litfasssaeulen* (pillars for posting news and advertisements), drawing small crowds. Questioning eyes met other questioning eyes. "Can that be true? Did you know?" Some people walked off in anger, rejecting the information as, "Lies, out-right lies!" Others rationalized that it was a practical impossibility to annihilate so many people. Numbers had grown into the millions. "Millions?" I asked myself also. "How can millions be killed without anybody knowing about it?" Not even my father, who listened regularly to the English radio broadcasts, had ever heard of 'death-camps' where prisoners were systematically being gassed and killed by the thousands. And the number of reported victims increased daily.

One of the worst places where such mass killings reportedly had taken place was Auschwitz. I had been there. Again and again, my mind revisited a scene on a dark, rainy November night in 1942 inside a huge, wire-fenced, heavily guarded compound—an underground factory, I was told. As a member of the dance company, I performed for the staff and workers there, and afterward attended a reception given by SS officers, a small group of older, balding, pudgy, cigar smoking men. Being sixteen, I was terribly bored.

After a short stay, I feigned a headache and asked to be taken back to our quarters. The duty to escort me past the many armed guards fell to a reluctant SS officer in his mid years. I wished it could have been anyone other than this man, whose features and demeanor was repulsively crude. He spit when he talked, and the fingers on his hands looked like puffed-up sausages.

It was pitch black outside. With only a flashlight to light the way, we sloshed through the soggy ground of the compound and braced against wind-whipped rain and sleet. Neither of us seemed in the mood for conversation. In the distance, I saw floodlights, and as we came closer, I saw a row of men—ten or more—digging.

"What in the world are they doing in the middle of this dark, cold, stormy night?" I broke the silence, my curiosity getting the best of me. While I did not expect a rational explanation—we were, after all, in a top-secret place—I was unprepared for his answer.

"Oh, these are just a bunch of Jews digging their own graves," he said casually, as if it were a common occurrence.

"Figures," I thought. "That looks just like him to make a brutish comment like this."

It simply confirmed my impression of him. I attributed his callous remark to his obvious resentment of having to get out in this weather to walk me back to my barracks, and that he meant to shock me. In retrospect, I asked myself many times how I could have been so naïve, so dense, and still shudder what I might have said or done had I taken his sarcastic remark seriously, and what the consequences might have been.

The list of accusations grew. War crimes Germany was accused of included the mass murders in Russia, in the Katyn Forest near Smolensk, where thousands of Polish officers and soldiers had been found executed and dumped in shallow mass graves. I was in Smolensk, entertaining German troops, when this massacre was discovered in the spring of 1943. Everybody, from the German general to the common soldier seemed genuinely horrified by this gruesome find. There was absolutely no doubt that these men had been executed by the Russians. I could still hear the frustrated German general, trying in vain to summon an international committee to inspect the site, say to his adjutant, "The Allies want to shove this into our shoes." He was right. The Allies, who had refused to be a witness, now did accuse the Germans of these murders. That made me question just how many of their other claims were false, also. I did not know anymore what or whom to believe.

A Nazi manhunt began. Amis made arrests. One day, as I sat again by the window watching Ami guards pace back and forth, I saw two Ami soldiers scuffle with a man, dragging him up the street. As they came closer, I recognized the Nazi party's district leader. Handcuffed, arms behind his back, he protested vigorously and resisted. One soldier with a club used it on him repeatedly and with open contempt. My stomach knotted. I knew this man. I had been at his house several times when my father had to answer to charges that he spoke out against the war, or against the Hitler regime, or failed to salute and display the Nazi flag. Instead of having my father arrested, as he was supposed to do, this man only read the charges to him, followed by a wink and a warning to be more careful in the future. He closed the file, and that was that. We owed this man our gratitude, quite possibly even my father's life.

"They are arresting Herr...(I have forgotten his name). We must do something!" I called out in panic. Only my mother was home at the time, and when she saw that I intended to rush out there, she snatched my shoes and blocked my way. "You stay here. There is nothing you can do. You'll just make trouble for us."

"We must help him. He has helped us," I countered. We struggled and argued back and forth.

"They will arrest you right along with him," she finally said and broke into tears. "Don't you care about us? Don't you care what this would do to us if something happened to you?"

I gave up. By that time, the men had turned the corner and disappeared. Not a single soul came to this man's defense. I felt sick with guilt.

When I told my father later, he did not even look up. He just said with a sigh, "Nothing ever changes."

I noticed how people curtained off their thoughts again, carefully choosing every word, and how they eyed one another with suspicion. Once again, anyone bent on vengeance could get another into serious trouble, only now by tagging this person a "Nazi."

In the world press, the word Nazi became fused to concentration camp murders and any and all other atrocities committed under Hitler's tyrannical rule. It became a buzzword, used indiscriminately to deride, accuse and condemn.

Nazi. The meaning of the word evolved from simply denoting a political party, the National Socialists Workers Party and its followers. In the course of the party's often violent political struggle, the meaning of

Nazi shifted to tag mostly the thugs of this party. Later, it became the label for its feared fanatical members who would have their own mothers shot for speaking out against Hitler. After the war, the meaning of 'Nazi' and 'German' became blurred, mentioned in the same breath, carelessly or consciously.

As the genocidal, evil intent and the executions by the Nazi regime came to light, it did not seem to shock my father as much as it did most other people. It did not surprise him that this could happen in the twentieth century, and in a civilized, advanced nation like Germany, a nation that prided itself for being a leader in the world of arts and sciences. At that time, I did not fully understand his quiet, passive acceptance of these events, events that made my blood curdle and spring-loaded my impatience to act. However, I guessed that his attitude was based on his experiences.

From birth, my father had been the victim of governmental, communal and social policies that subjected him to inconceivable brutality and hardships. Under the King, his mother and father had been denied permission to marry, though his mother was already with child. His father stood in the King's service to become a forest ranger, as was his father and father's father before him. His mother was a poor farmer's daughter, working as a housemaid at a mountain lodge in Bavaria, casting her several classes below a forest ranger's status. Neither of them had money to declare their independence, nor did they have the support from family and a cast-conscious, catholic society. Thus, my father was born under the stigma of illegitimacy—a bastard child—and his mother stood disgraced as a sinner of the worst kind by having a child out of wedlock. To escape her shame, she fled into a marriage with a man she hardly knew, and placed Josef, her infant son with her sickly parents. When my father was about four years old, his beloved grandmother passed away. His grandfather, too sick to care for him, persuaded the boy's mother to come and take him. She lived with her husband in Swabia, far away from her birthplace in lower Bavaria.

From a poor but caring environment, little Josef fell into the hands of his cruel, jealous stepfather, who resented his very existence. Suffering beating after beating, he finally ran away. A gendarme found him crouched in an alley, black and blue and crying. Seeing the bruises on the child's face and body, the police arrested his stepfather and threw him in jail. A year or so later, when his stepfather was released, he was angrier than ever. Finally, Josef was removed from the home and returned to his very ill grandfather who died shortly afterwards. Now, Josef became a ward of the county.

All this time, his natural father had diligently paid child support, but could not or would not take over the physical care of his son. Until a home could be found for the child, these payments now flowed into county coffers, and the appointed county officials responsible for finding the boy a home, quickly figured out that if someone would take the boy for less money than what his father paid in child support, they could keep the rest. Thus, they decided to auction the little 'bastard' off to the lowest bidder. The lowest bidder happened to be the poorest farmer, looking for a cheap, extra pair of hands.

From this day forth, my father was put to work in the fields, cleaning the stable, herding livestock, and doing many other chores around the farm. For this he received food—a diet of bread and cabbage or turnip soup—and a bed of straw in a loft to sleep on. For the slightest transgressions, or for not performing as expected, he received beatings with a leather strap. Because the farmer had accepted the boy for just a minimal payment from the county, villagers thought of him as a Good Samaritan for taking the little 'bastard' in.

The village priest became my father's only friend. He insisted that he be sent to school, and to Sunday mass, and he made him an altar boy, whereby he raised his lowly status. Still, my father remained the whipping boy for what ever went wrong in the village. Once, a deliveryman lost his money satchel; my father was accused of stealing it. When a window got broken, or a horse bolted, my father was blamed. Though facts later revealed that he was innocent, it would never be acknowledged.

In school, he fared no better. His male teacher whipped him with a bamboo stick for things he never did. "Why did you not tell this to the priest?" I asked whenever he told me about his brutal youth. "At that time, boys were raised by the strap," my father explained. This was a commonly accepted practice. But my father also harbored a dark secret he was too ashamed to share. He was a bed-wetter.

One day during the coldest part of winter, a mailman walked by the railroad tracks where some coaches sat idle. He observed a small, thawed spot on an icy window. Thinking that, perhaps, a transient had sought shelter inside this coach, he stopped to investigate. What he found was a barely conscious and frozen young boy. He picked him up and carried him to the house of a school teacher, who immediately wrapped the child in blankets, put him next to the stove, and spooned him warm milk. The boy was my father, who once again had run away from his abuser.

Outraged, after having pried the story out of Josef, and seeing the welts and bruises on his body, the teacher issued a complaint against the county and the people responsible for such unconscionable abuse.

From then on, my father's life took a turn for the better. He was placed with a family who treated him kindly. Still, in society's eyes he remained a seed of sin.

These early experiences, of which my father talked only rarely, had left their indelible mark. Most of his tormentors had been church-going Christians, pillars of the community, under the eye of church and state, while the rest of society had its head stuck in the sand. My father entertained no illusions about the world. Life would go on as it always had: good for some, and bad for others.

In spite of his cruel upbringing, my father was gentle. He abhorred violence. Thus, he became a pacifist, with traces of contempt for any officialdom and for society in general. He had no ambition to climb the ladder of success—referring to it as *"Eine Huehnerleiter"* (chicken ladder)—preferring to live quietly, helping friends and neighbors when in need. Yet, he stubbornly clung to his principles.

With the revelation about Nazi atrocities, my attitude about my father's political stand shifted. Perhaps, he was right all along not to have joined the Nazi party. Perhaps, all the years we had spent in fear and poverty, deprived of economic and other opportunities allowed us now to emerge with a clear conscience on the side of justice and human decency. Suddenly, I found cause to be proud of my father, and even went so far as to count him and us victors of this war against tyranny and oppression.

Oh, what pompous delusions! It was a bubble destined to burst. Sure, Hitler was dead; and his regime had been defeated, but that would neither change nor bring peace or justice to the world. It simply removed one madman and one fanatical, brutal regime. The age-old laws and rules prevailed: "Might makes right." My father understood this.

◆　◆　◆

Times were extremely hard. People in the cities literally starved to death. Children begged under the windows and along fences of GI housing for food, cigarettes, chocolate, and chewing gum. Young mothers, their husbands dead or missing, sacrificed respect and accepted the attention of American men who helped feed their starving broods.

Because of our two GI friends, Bob and Harry, we scraped by. Even so, our meals often consisted of dandelion soup and a slice of bread, or a field salad and boiled potatoes. We seldom had leftovers, but when we did, in the summer's heat, without refrigeration, the food turned sour over night. My father ate it anyway. It was too precious to waste. When we did cook a piece of meat or fry a slice of Spam, we had to close all windows so that the aroma would not drift outside and further incite our neighbors' envy.

Feeling safe enough now to venture beyond our immediate neighborhood, my father and I hopped on our bikes to check on friends. We gasped when we saw for the first time the total devastation caused by the last mass bombings. Some areas were destroyed beyond recognition. We could no longer tell what street we were on. Hollow, jagged brick walls, piles of rubble and twisted debris were all that remained of the four and five story buildings with shops and apartments, where many of my schoolmates had lived. A modest breeze stirred up bits of paper and ash to perform a macabre dance above the ruins, filling the air with dust and the stench of charred remains.

Amazingly, amidst this total devastation, the Agfa factory where I had been forced to work until days before the occupation, remained standing as if singled out with surgical precision. As most factories, the Agfa had been converted to manufacture arms, which classified it as a strategic target. But because bombs had missed it and other such industrial complexes—intentionally or by coincidence—it fueled speculations that American interests were involved. This, and the systematic blanket-bombing of residential areas in which thousands of civilians perished or lost their homes, discredited the Allies, whose propaganda claimed that all they had wanted was to stop Hitler, destroy his war machine, and liberate the German people. What it accomplished was to solidify the German people behind its leaders. What else? Whom could they trust? Whom could they believe? And where and to whom could they turn?

From day one of the war, my father had listened regularly to the English broadcasts. We owned a powerful *Telefunken* radio with short-wave channels, a luxury of questionable legality, and the only luxury my father had ever afforded himself. For him, it was like an only window, a window to the world. With the radio turned down low, with ears only inches from the speaker, he listened to news from the other side. Somewhere between its propaganda and ours, he sought to piece together a realistic picture and keep track of advancing and retreating armies.

"Someday, somebody finds out that you listen to the English sender and take you away," my mother warned and fretted. She wanted no part of this.

Occasionally I listened in, but what I heard only angered me. "The Allies say they are our friends?" I jeered. "Our friends? Night and day, their bombers turn our cities into a blazing hell. Then, as if that is not enough, their planes dive down and machine-gun those fleeing the inferno. They make sport of gunning down

32

peaceful farmers plowing their fields. And they have the gall to call themselves our friends?" I paused, almost frothing at the mouth. "Is it a wonder why Germans rally behind Hitler? Is he worse than they or their friend and ally, Stalin?" As I saw it, the English broadcasts were a bunch of rubbish, no different from the propaganda the German radio put out.

Once war is declared, a line is drawn that pits brother against brother if they happen to wind up on opposite sides. And always, ordinary people do the suffering, bleeding and dying for the policies and reckless decisions their leaders make.

It was best not to think back. The war was over now. At least the air raids and the killing had stopped. What tomorrow would bring was anybody's guess. In the struggle of day-to-day survival, the future lay in the next slice of bread or shovel full of coal. It was as simple as that.

◆   ◆   ◆

On the way to my girlfriend's house, my father and I pedaled through sections of town damaged by some of the first air raids on Munich. From the heaps of crumbling walls, broken brick and twisted metal, bright yellow dandelions poked their heads. They beamed like miniature suns from the rubble and coaxed a brief smile to my face. Nature had already started to rebuild; maybe, so could we. These lowly flowers carried a message of hope and encouragement. Life would continue.

When we arrived at my girlfriend's apartment, Mama Mueller opened the door. She appeared thinner than ever. A fleeting smile flashed across her face, followed by sobs and a flood of tears. She gestured us inside, wiping her eyes with the corner of her faded flowered apron.

33

"What is wrong?" I asked, alarmed.

Entering the kitchen-living room, my friend Hanni and her younger sister, Gitta, sat by the window, mending clothes. Hanni dropped her sewing and greeted me with a hug. Gitta said hello. Both girls had been crying, also.

"It's Michel," Mama Mueller explained. "He lies badly wounded somewhere. We don't know where, or if he is still alive." Michel was her oldest son. She went on to tell us that one of his comrades came by earlier that day, wanting to know how he was doing, saying that he saw him being loaded onto a Red Cross transport.

"First it's Ernst, now Michel," Mama Mueller sobbed. Ernst, the younger of the two boys, was missing in action.

I asked about Albert, a friend of theirs and mine, who was drafted the same time Ernst was.

"He is dead. Killed in action," Hanni told me.

I remembered when he and Ernst had been called to war. Some friends had gathered at the Mueller's place to give them a rowdy send-off. We partied until the neighbors complained about the noise. The oldest in our group was seventeen. I was fourteen. Bursting with life and youthful optimism, no one had given serious thought that war was about killing and dying. While boys saw war as an adventure, mothers cried, and fathers bit their lips, remembering the First World War and those who did not return.

Papa Mueller came up from the basement with a basket full of debudded, shriveled potatoes. He and my father shook hands, but neither one seemed to know what to say to the other. Political opposites, they had on occasion butted heads. Papa Mueller had been a strong supporter of Hitler and remained loyal to him almost to the end. "Hitler has done all right by me," I had heard him say many times.

What did it matter now? Right or wrong, we all had lost.

Everywhere we went, we heard equally sad and tragic stories. Somehow, people carried on. With buckets, picks and shovels, citizens—women, children and old men—cleared the streets. They salvaged and repaired what they could. Makeshift stands popped up. Former shop owners and entrepreneurs traded skills and imagination in place of goods, sometimes over, sometimes under the table. The black market flourished. A shoemaker and once storeowner sold sandals made of wood and straw, and repaired shoes with leather salvaged from other old and worn-out items. At another place, a man soldered holes in leaking pots and pans. Other stands offered hand-made brooms and baskets, flowers, and newspapers. It was a modest beginning. For me, however, nothing would ever be the same again. Gone were the landmarks of my childhood, the school I went to, the church where I was confirmed, and the candy store where we kids spent our pennies after school. Gone were the homes of many of my friends where I had spent happy hours. Worse, gone were my friends. Some were dead, others had scattered to wherever they could find a roof to share. The ties to my childhood, my youth had been cut. I had lost my sense of home. The mere thought of it brings tears to my eyes even now.

Mitzi, Bob, and Hanni.

First two Americans - Bob and Harry and a buddy.

Girlfriend Hanni and I in our kitchen.

Mama and Papa by the radio.

Brother Willy training for the Olympics.

With my mother in 1944 in front
of kitchen window and air raid
shelter below.

In front of air raid shelter,
1944.

Mama, 1925.

Mitzi - 6 years old, on stage.

Singer Sefi, 1943.

Costume made from Nazi flag, 1945

Dance parody.

Mama in Bavarian dress, 1920.

Mitzi dancing the Skaters' Waltz, age 7.

Production of "Struwelpeter" - Mitzi second from left, dancing "Paulinchen"

41

Deutsche Theater - Munich, 1940 - second from left.

Deutsche Theater - Munich - Finale.

Chapter 3

Dancing for the Americans

    Summer stood in full bloom. The city of Munich limped slowly back to life. Trains and streetcars ran again on sporadic schedules, and temporary repairs restored electricity, gas and water lines to some parts of town.

Three months into the American occupation, we had a surprise visit from Sefi, a long time friend of my parents and a singer by profession. She came all the way from Tegernsee, a resort town in the Alps, about 30 miles south of Munich. Many such little towns and villages and its residents had survived the war quite well.

In her early forties, Sefi looked enviably groomed and chic, from her veiled pillbox hat down to her silk-stockinged legs and polished leather pumps. I could not take my eyes off her and listened intently as she told us over coffee—real coffee that she had brought with her—that she sang for the Amis now and as pay received food and cigarettes.

"You could do that, too. You could dance for them," she said to me. "Do you want to?"

"Do I want to! Yes, of course!" I answered without hesitation. "But I have no costumes, no shoes, no music..." My voice trailed off as my mind raced ahead. I saw opportunity, hope, a life. Whatever the obstacles, I had to overcome them somehow.

Even before Sefi had left, I had started to rummage through Mama's old trunks and suitcases where she kept bits and pieces of my old costumes from years ago, and vintage dresses from my grandmother, and where I had hidden the Nazi flag. Later, I cranked up our old phonograph and played every record we had. In my head, at least, emerged a plan and the beginning of a repertoire.

"Think about it, performing for the Amis. See what you can come up with," Sefi said in parting. "I'll check back with you in a few weeks."

The very next day, I asked around for a creative seamstress and heard about a widow in the neighborhood who did mending and sewing for people. She did good work, her clients said. However, making costumes for the stage required a little more than just neat stitching. But, what did I have to lose? I looked her up.

Frau Klara lived and worked in one room in someone else's apartment. The government had placed her there after she had lost her home in an air raid. The room, kept neat and clean, had a daybed, a wardrobe, a commode, a large table and a wood stove on which she could do limited cooking and heat her iron. Under the only window stood a treadle sewing machine and chair.

Standing just inside her door, I introduced myself and said that one of her clients had referred me to her. "I've heard good things about your work and wonder..."

We sized each other up. She was short and noticeably deformed. One shoulder was lower than the other and bulged out in back, forming a hump. It was clearly visible under her gray cotton frock.

"I am a dancer," I started to explain. "I need somebody who can sew a few costumes for me, somebody with imagination, who can work from an idea. I have made a few sketches..." I was about to hand her the small roll of papers when I suddenly realized what I was asking and expecting from this woman. My arm dropped limp to my side. Frau Klara's face remained expressionless.

"I guess, I'm asking too much. You are probably too busy anyway," I said, ready to retreat.

"Won't you come in and sit down," she said. "Let me have a look at your sketches."

She is just being polite, I thought, but I complied. Bent over my drawings, she pursed her lips and nodded slightly. When she looked up, something about her had changed. Her face seemed illuminated as if a light had turned on inside her head.

"It's been years since anything challenged my skill or imagination. Mending, alterations, that's all I've been doing."

"I have no patterns, only these rough sketches of what I want," I said to her.

"That's no problem," she replied. "By when do you need these costumes?"

"As soon as possible."

We talked a while longer. She reminisced about how much she had enjoyed creating costumes for people during the carnival (Mardi Gras) season—a time of blissful madness before the war.

As agreed upon, next day she came to my place. Together we examined every remnant and bits and pieces of old clothes and costumes in my mother's trunk. When I showed her the flag, intended for a Spanish costume, she excitedly volunteered suggestions. "We can use the black of the swastika for trim around a ruffled skirt, then take this black, beaded georgette from this 1920's dress to make a bolero for it, maybe even a small mantilla."

We sat on the floor in front of that musty old trunk, stuff scattered everywhere, passing ideas back and forth faster than the wag of an excited dog's tail. My mother looked quietly on for a while then left the room. I did not realize then how left out and hurt she must have felt. Before now, it was always she who had designed and made my costumes. I had been the entire focus of her life, slipping away now, no longer consulting her, no longer needing her. Where had the years gone to? However, both of us understood that my requirements now were beyond her ability.

Mama grew up as the granddaughter of a wealthy patrician in the service of the King. Girls born to this station were expected to conform to the standards of that class, to be devout, chaste, frugal, and always dignified. No frills. But she was a highly spirited child, with a lust for life, stifled by the dictates of her time and place. She inherited her spirit from her father, a master craftsman, a man with flair, who had married into this patrician family. He understood and loved his youngest daughter, my mother, who liked to primp and pose in front of a mirror; who liked to play dress-up and games of pretend; who wished for nothing more than to be on stage someday. Tragically, her father fell ill and died as Mama reached her teens. Too much to handle for her mother, Mama was placed in the care of ultra strict nuns for the last years of her schooling, where she learned to sew and do fine needlework. At age eighteen, an attention-getting beauty, she followed her two older sisters to the United States. She stayed and worked in the USA, and became engaged to a wealthy businessman, until her mother became very ill and she felt obligated to return home. She never made it back.

Mama's life could be best described as that of a show horse hitched to a plow. Mama was already in her thirties when she met my father. War, inflation, and unresolved disputes with her family left her penniless, alone and disillusioned. The pain of their pasts drew my parents together into a loving relationship that lasted a lifetime. My father adored my mother, but could offer her only a meager existence. Mama's early dreams lay dormant and forgotten until I came along. Her dreams revived, and I was to fulfill them. She wanted to give me what she could not have.

That evening, after Sefi's visit, Mama and I sat in the kitchen way past midnight, separating the black and white emblem from the flag's center, carefully pulling and saving every bit of thread for use later on. Mama reminisced about my performances as a child, and the many costumes she had sewn for me, as if these times had been the happiest in her life.

Early the next day, I took everything over to Frau Klara, who immediately went to work taking my measurements.

"I will need some spools of red or black thread," she said, adding, "I have enough to get started but it won't go far."

"Thread for the sewing machine? Oh, my! I had not even thought of it," I said. "Where in the world can I find and buy spools of thread?"

"I know a place...people from whom I used to buy my supplies. I am sure I still could get some from them, but they want more than money now."

"How about a few cigarettes?"

"That would do."

47

On my way home from Frau Klara's place, I thought of so many more things I needed: shoes for the stage, records, phonograph needles, sheet music. It seemed overwhelming. How would I get all of it together?

Papa let me have a few cigarettes our Ami friends had given him and smoked the tobacco saved from left-over butts instead. Mama was less cooperative. I asked if we could spare a can of Spam. The cans were small, containing no more than a couple of tablespoons full. "No," she said firmly. She was in one of her moods. Later, I saw her feed some to her cat—a beautiful, pure-bred Angora.

Since I had not danced or worked out for over a year, my muscles had shrunk; my body had stiffened. Getting back in shape was a struggle in itself, but I also had a very painful type of arthritis causing inflammation and swelling in my joints. The pain was so severe at times that Mama had to help me out of bed in the morning. It let up after I took aspirin and moved around for a while.

I cleared an area in my room, cranked up the old phonograph, selected a record for a Spanish dance and began to practice. With a pair of castanets and in my only pair of shoes, I choreographed a fiery flamenco number.

When Sefi came again a few weeks later, I had one dance number and costume, and was working on two others. Frau Klara had outdone herself on the Spanish costume and already pieced together something for two other costumes. Papa, who had collected dues for an insurance company during the last years of the war, scrounged up a pair of used silver sandals for me from one of his many clients. I still needed sheet music and approached a music teacher in the neighborhood. Bombed-out, he lived with his wife and four children in a single room and was in dire need of ev-

48

erything. For a couple of cans of sardines and a few cigarettes, he was willing to transfer and hand-copy the music from record to paper, and even orchestrate it for the various instruments of a small orchestra.

Miraculously, everything fell into place. I had three dance numbers now and Sefi got me my first job at a former convalescent home in a suburb of Munich, which served as temporary housing for people liberated and recuperating from labor camps and Nazi prisons. My touring experience, especially six months on the Russian front, had taught me to improvise, adapt and perform under just about any condition. However, my debut was less than professional, but the audience applauded and I received 120.00 Reichsmarks and a three-course dinner, of which I stuffed half into my pockets to take home. After some rough starts and stops, I signed with an agent who put shows together for the Special Service, and who booked me into American clubs and bases. Oh, was I in for a culture shock!

The first time I stepped out in front of a GI audience, whistles and shouts of "Hubba-hubba!" and "Take it off...take it off," drowned out the music from the record player. I did not understand what their yelling meant. Was it a sign of approval or disapproval? American soldiers behaved so very differently than German soldiers. Never once had I heard them whistle and yell. They clapped and stamped their feet to show approval, and booed when they did not like a performance, though that had never happened to me. Sometimes Russians in our audiences whistled and threw coins onto the stage to show approval. So, perhaps, this was the American way. I glanced at my agent standing next to the stage, operating the record player. He beamed and gestured to go on with my number. "They liked you. They liked you," he told me afterwards.

I soon noticed that the GI's rowdy outbursts were directed not just at me, but at all young female performers. But when I finally learned the meaning of their raucous chants, I was devastated. Why did I train and practice hours each day trying to perfect my numbers when all the GI's really wanted was a striptease?

In the beginning, my agent occasionally booked a concert pianist, violinist or flutist as part of our show, most of them celebrity artists. At best, GI audiences tolerated them like background music in a cocktail bar. At worst, they booed them off the stage. It hurt. My colleagues and I could not understand. We actually felt the need to apologize to these artists for the Americans' bad behavior. Many nights I came home and cried myself to sleep.

The pay was good, usually including one or two packs of cigarettes, which was a fortune. With cigarettes one could buy anything on the black market, and we needed so much. Like it or not, I had to continue working for the Amis. And I kept on training to satisfy my own standards and, at least, earn the respect from my colleagues and countrymen.

As badly as GIs behaved as an audience, as individuals, most of them treated us kindly, with courtesy and respect. Ironically, in officers' clubs, this was often the reverse. The audiences behaved better, but individually, quite a few officers did not behave like gentlemen.

One of the early shows took place at an officers club in Dachau. An army truck had picked up our agent, and in turn all the people in the show, one by one, from all over Munich. Later, they would take us home the same way. We had no control over when we arrived, or when we returned home. That particular day we had arrived early and had to wait in a small room until show time. Officially, Americans were still not

allowed to fraternize with Germans, though most ignored this rule. That day it was strictly enforced. As
we sat around waiting, talking, three officers came
bursting in and ordered us to come with them.

"Come...mach schnell...schnell...we'll show you
what you Germans did."

Their threatening tone and demeanor frightened us.
We thought we were under arrest. They herded us
outside, onto a truck, and drove us a few miles to the
Dachau concentration camp. The arched entrance still
displayed Hitler's motto in big letters: "Arbeit macht
frei (work makes free)." Inside, they ordered us off
the truck and to fall in line with other German civilians—including children—to tour the compound. We
had to file through the coops where prisoners had slept
in filthy bunks stacked shelf-like from floor to ceiling,
worse than any stable. In an adjacent cement stall,
dried, splattered blood stained walls and ceiling.

"That's where you bludgeoned your victims to
death," the guide said.

In the yard stood whipping poles on which knotted leather lashes and whips for flogging hung on display. Past that, we saw a pile of dirt and ashes with
bones and partial human skulls. Women in our line
turned their heads and shielded their children's eyes
from these grisly sights.

"You look," the Americans demanded. "Look, so
you will never forget what you Germans, you barbarians did to the Jews."

"We didn't do this. Why do they accuse us?" I muttered under my breath to the person standing next to
me.

People in the line looked frightened. Many bowed
their heads, some placed a handkerchief over their
mouth to stifle their gasps, others seemed close to faint-

ing, but the Americans forced us to go on, to look and endure.

Suddenly a thought hit me like a boulder. "This is where my father would have landed, had it not been for our neighbor, the SA leader, the man the Amis had arrested." I swallowed hard. A mix of emotions from gratitude, to resentment lumped up in my throat.

Next, our guides herded us through the offices of former camp officials, pointing out lampshades they said were made from human skin, and shrunken heads of former prisoners. It was hard to believe that this was for real.

At every turn, these Americans lashed at us with words of contempt as if WE had been the perpetrator of these vile, inhuman deeds. I doubt if any among us had had knowledge, much less a hand in what went on inside these walls. Instead of allowing us to mourn the victims who had been imprisoned there, these officers pierced our hearts with spikes of their hate. It bred resentment. Personally, I felt not only insulted, I was deeply wounded and alarmed to be lumped in with torturers and assassins. Do other Americans think and react like these officers? I wondered.

When we returned to the club, our troupe was so traumatized and upset that we did not think we could perform that evening. Our agent pulled his hair. "If you don't go on, they won't give us transportation home. What do you suggest we do? Walk home twenty, thirty miles in the middle of night? So they can arrest us for breaking the curfew?" He paced back and forth in front of us, then disappeared again, trying to negotiate a truce.

"Why do they even want us to stay? I would think they'd be glad to get rid of us barbarians," the drummer of our band called out after him. Most of us sat around in a quiet, sunken heap, like rag dolls from which the stuffing had fallen out.

When our agent reappeared, he brought with him the club's manager. I assumed he was an officer, too. "Look," he addressed us, taking a broad-legged stance, "I'll give everybody an extra pack of cigarettes. Just do the show. I'll be in very hot water if you don't."

"Scheiss auf Deine Zigaretten," the drummer responded, "stick them up your ass!"

"Look, we have to do something," one of the other musicians suggested timidly. "I am thinking of my wife and kids. They'll be worried out of their minds if I don't come home tonight."

How worried my parents would be, had crossed my mind, also.

"Let's just do the show and get it over with," someone else suggested.

Finally, we resolved to do the show. The club manager breathed an obvious sigh of relief. "You can order anything you want from the bar. I'll send in a waiter," he said.

We unpacked and got ready. A young fellow came in, wearing a bar apron. "I'll take your orders. What do you want to drink?" he asked in German.

"German waiters? Here...?" The drummer reacted with surprise. "How did you come to work for them?"

"Your order, please," the waiter replied. Glancing back over his shoulders, he added in a whisper, "I am not allowed to talk to you. I'm a prisoner of war. The waiters, the band—we all are."

The drinks he brought us were potent and helped to dull our feelings. I could not finish mine. One of the musicians did it for me.

Every time the door to our dressing room opened, sounds of a gypsy violin drifted in. I loved Gypsy music, regarding it as the song of a human heart because of its range of emotions: joyful and sweet one moment, sad or angry the next. It also reminded me of Pepi and romantic summer evenings under a star-studded Russian sky.

It was showtime. Our musicians dragged their instruments through aisles between crowded tables in the packed, smoke-filled clubroom to set up. The rest of us stretched our necks to see the floor on which we had to perform, how big and how slick it was.

A medley of American tunes by our five-man band started the program. It included a drum and saxophone solo, and a wild boogie-woogie on the piano to warm up the audience. I was next. With a frozen smile, my body performed what it was rehearsed to do. I could not, however, infuse it with the sparkle and spirit of the music, a Lehar waltz. Within me still raged a storm of emotions. My second number, a lively Spanish dance in my red Nazi-flag costume went better. It allowed me to express my defiance and rage. Head held high, my heels hammered the floor and my castanets clicked sharper than ever. The audience loved it. That evening it was polite.

After the performance, a waiter delivered a message to me from a general, asking me to join him at his table. I was in no mood that night to party, or fraternize with Americans, but was lured by the sounds of the gypsy violin drifting again into the dressing room.

"Go ahead," my agent encouraged and winked at me. "I'll call you when it's time to leave."

I followed the waiter to the general's table. The general rose, and so did the other officers with him and offered me a chair.

"I enjoyed your dancing and wanted to meet you," the general, a man in his sixties, said. I thanked him and sat down, surprised to be shown such courtesy.

"What would you like to drink?"

I opted for a soda. It was all my empty stomach could handle.

My English vocabulary had expanded enough to allow me to engage in a simple conversation. Actually, I had learned many words that were not even in my small schoolbook dictionary.

The violinist, a lean, dark-haired, dark eyed young man, wandered over to our table, playing a tune I often had heard Pepi play. He had the same charming style. A lump formed in my throat and I swallowed hard to keep from breaking into tears. I still could not accept that Pepi was dead.

"Is there something special you want him to play?" the general asked me.

I shook my head. "Whatever he wants to play."

"All right, then. Play something nice for the lady," the General ordered.

The fellow snapped to attention, "Jawohl, Herr General," and began to play a gypsy love song from a Lehar operetta. I closed my eyes. Memories flooded my head and heart. I could almost hear Pepi's voice, and feel his touch.

"Well done," the General complimented the young man after he had finished. "What's your name?"

"Chicosh, Herr General."

"Thank you, Chicosh," I said.

Chicosh bowed. Our eyes met and lingered briefly in woeful recognition of our demoted state. I wished I could have talked with him.

Our show was ready to leave. "Where do you live?" the general asked. I explained as best as I could. "That seems to be right on my way. Why don't you let me take you home?"

I hesitated. Through my head ran thoughts like, "He is a nice older man, older than my father. He is a general. Surely, I would be safe with him, and I would not have to ride all over Munich on the back of a truck, always the last one to be dropped off."

"Thank you. That would be nice," I accepted.

A German prisoner helped load my suitcase with costumes into the trunk of the general's car. "You hooked yourself a big fish, even if he is a little old for you," he said to me out of one side of his mouth. "You know, of course, that he is the temporary Governor of Bavaria."

I did not know that, but I knew what the fellow was thinking. What could I say? How could I defend myself? And why should I have to? I let it slide.

The general opened the car door for me and I slid into the front seat. Everything about his car was ultimate luxury, from the soft leather upholstery to a built-in bar. He proudly showed it off, explaining the purpose of every knob and button. It had just recently arrived from the States. With the radio turned low, I could not even hear the engine. The car seemed to float on air. I felt like a queen.

Scum of the earth one minute, a queen the next. Being exposed frequently to such extremes fractured my identity like glass exposed to extreme heat and cold. What and who am I? Where did I belong?

On the way home, the general asked me polite questions about my career, where and how long I had studied and where I had danced. When we arrived at my place, he saw me to the door, kissed my hand and said he would like to see me again. Enormously flattered, doubting, however, that he really meant it, I said yes and thanked him for the ride in his fabulous car. It crossed my mind how helpful it could be to befriend such an important person.

The general actually did call on me again a week or two later, and I became his guest at various gala events. One of the first was a party at his residence, a beautiful villa that once belonged to some Nazi big shot. He sent his driver to pick me up.

Neighbors, who monitored my comings and goings from behind curtained windows to gossip about it later, did not miss a beat. I saw their curtains moving again this time and snickered. Now, I really had given them something to talk about.

I wore the only good dress I owned, a long-sleeved black crepe with my only pair of patched, worn-out blue oxfords. At the party, I mingled with stars of the German screen and stage, and high ranking Ami officers, all dressed in their finest. I felt like Cinderella minus a fairy godmother, a 'nobody,' accepted only because I was the general's guest, who introduced me as "tomorrow's star."

Most Germans present also spoke better English than I. My teachers were the American GIs. During a conversation, in which I wanted to convey how angry I was about something, I used an expression I frequently heard the Amis use: "...and I was so pissed off."

Instantly, the room full of guests fell silent. All eyes focused on me.

"Oh, my! Did I say something wrong?" I asked, placing both hands over my mouth.

"You used language unbefitting a young lady as yourself," the general corrected me in a kind, fatherly tone of voice.

"Oh, I am so sorry, General, please forgive me. But what, exactly, did I say that was so bad?"

"Some other time. I can't explain it to you now," he said.

"It was that awful what I've said?"

The General nodded.

"Oh, I apologize, General, but it's what I hear your soldiers say all the time when they are angry. If it's that bad, maybe you should have a talk with them. I learn my English from them."

"You have a point there." He chuckled. "I guess we must excuse you."

Now everybody laughed. The guests all had a story of their own to tell about their troubles with a foreign language. This incident added much to the sport of the evening.

I had felt safe and protected in the general's company. Therefore it came as a complete shock when later, on a tour through the house, he propositioned me. He seemed amused as I oohed and aahed at the modernistic elegance of this villa, from the book filled library with its luxurious leather furniture, to the marble bathrooms and the king-sized bed and room-sized, mirrored closets in the bedrooms.

"How would you like to share this with me?" he said, with a sheepish grin, gesturing toward his bed. I could not believe that he meant what he implied. Ignoring what he said, I turned to leave the room. He reached for my shoulder and turned me around to face him. "Well?" he said. "You would have it good."

I stared at him. At this instant, he diminished in my eyes from a general to just a man, and an old man at that. "You are old enough to be my father. Perhaps, even old enough to be my grandfather," I said, totally perplexed and caught off guard.

Still grinning, he reacted with a nod, drew up his mouth and tightened his chin, then led the way downstairs. I was not frightened but felt awkward and did not know how to react. He called his driver to take me home. I was already in the car when he asked me, "May I still see you now and then?"

I shrugged my shoulders. "Perhaps. Why not?"

I felt we had reached an understanding, but I never took for granted again that old men were a safe bet.

Chapter 4

Puzzling and Contrary

For some time already, I had wondered why I saw so many black GIs on the streets of Munich, and never once saw one in the clubs where I performed. I was curious about them. To Germans, Negroes were a novelty. Finally, I came face to face with one. After performing at a small outfit, our show joined a group of men gathered around a piano. From their midst rose a big, rich baritone, singing arias from various operas. The sound of that beautiful voice flowed effortlessly out of the broad chest of a towering black man in army uniform. He sang in French, Italian, as well as in English. His voice was trained. This man was no amateur. We immediately thought that he was a big opera star in the States, and asked him later if, perhaps, he had sung in the famous Met in New York.

He burst out laughing. "Opera houses in the States have no call for black baritones."

Baffled, we asked, "Well, where do you sing?"

"In church. At weddings and funerals."

As we talked further, we learned that he was the unit's cook and, once his tour of duty was up, he planned to live in France, where he stood a better chance to join an opera company. That seemed odd to us. We deduced that Americans just had no appreciation for opera.

Not long after this encounter, I was booked with a show to Lake *Walchensee*, one of the most scenic places in the Alps, and the site of a power plant that supplied Munich with electricity and water. My father, working in a labor camp for a year, helped build it. I fondly recalled the strolls my mother and I took along the deep blue water of the lake as we visited him. In the spring and summer, we picked arms full of wildflowers that colored the sloping meadows. I especially delighted in hearing my voice echo back and forth between the surrounding mountains. But now it was fall and the weather had turned raw. The water of the lake looked black. Clouds and fog obscured the peaks and muted every sound.

Our show arrived in a covered army truck at an all-black unit. We saw only black faces everywhere. "Night-fighters," we had heard them called. The black soldiers helped us unload and set up. They fed us. We commented on how very polite they all were. "Yes Ma'am. Yes Miss. Yes Sir." During our performance, they whistled and clapped, but not one of them shouted, "Take it off!" This totally amazed us. They were better behaved than all the rest of the Amis, including officers. We liked performing for them. These first impressions set the tone for how I viewed black people from then on.

Young German women who had befriended black soldiers confirmed our findings. They said that the black soldiers treated them like queens. However, when white soldiers saw them together on the street, they hurled insults and picked fights with them. Some

Germans soon picked up on that and called the women "*Negerweiber*" (Negro wench). After witnessing such incidents, I came home shaking my head, saying to my father, "I don't understand. First, it's the Jew, now it's the Negro who gets picked on, and nobody seems to object. I just don't understand."

I worked every weekend now. The routine was always the same; an army truck picked us up from where we lived, and brought us home, one after another. The driver, a GI, always carried a pass and trip ticket for all of us. Sometimes, MPs stopped the truck, checked the papers, then let us go on. One night, as only three musicians and I were left on the truck, MPs stopped us again. We did not think much of it until we heard the driver and two MPs get into an argument. Peeking out from the truck's canopy, we saw one MP tear up the driver's papers and toss them to the wind. "I just need a few more points for a furlough home to the States. The hell with those Krauts," he said to the driver. To us he said, "You are under arrest for breaking the curfew." Laughing at our sputtered protests, one MP replaced the driver, the other followed the truck in his jeep, and they hauled us off to a downtown jail in Munich. They muscled us inside—the musicians with their instruments, me with my suitcase full of costumes—then turned us over to the German police. Again, we protested our wrongful arrest, but the German staff only shrugged their shoulders. "Tell it to the judge," they said. They fingerprinted us, then searched us and our baggage for contraband. It was illegal to have anything American in one's possession. We all had a couple of packs of cigarettes with us, that night's pay for our show. Sweat pearled up on my forehead as they looked through my suitcase. Incredibly, maybe purposely, they overlooked them. I also had a broken pack of cigarettes in my purse, but they handed that back to me, too, without comment.

Wardens led us away, the two musicians in one direction, me in another. A woman warden put me in a cell with three drunken prostitutes. When the cell door slammed shut, the sound hit me like the bullet from a gun. My legs gave out under me. I collapsed onto one of the iron double bunks and buried my face in my hands.

"Must be your first time," one of the women said and laughed. "What did you do?"

"Nothing. I've done nothing." My voice faltered.

"Neither did we." She struck a helpless, pathetic pose. Her cellmates burst into hysterics and took turns acting the innocent victims.

"Quiet! Quiet," a male voice ordered, "or I'll put you in the hole."

A hard bang against the cell bars made me jump and look up. The women toned down. A male warden with a club in his hand threatened them with added jail time if they did not shut up.

He looked down at me, still sitting on the bunk, dejected, in a heap of despair, with tears streaming down my face. "What are you doing in there?" he said.

"I don't know," I sobbed and shook my head.

He unlocked the cell door and ordered me out. Shaking with fear, not knowing what to expect, I followed the warden across the jailhouse corridor to a cell with a solid door that had just a small, barred window in its center.

"Here," his voice sounded much softer now, "at least you can get a few hour's sleep in here. That's better than spending the night with those drunken floozies. What are you in for, anyway?"

His sympathetic tone calmed me enough that I could tell him what had happened. I could even gather enough courage to ask if I could smoke.

"Go ahead," he said.

I took the broken pack of cigarettes out of my purse. "Would you like one?" I offered. "Thanks," he said and pulled one out and stuck it in his shirt pocket.

Across from that cell was an alcove where a couple of other wardens sat, playing cards.

"Hey!" they called to him. "Do you want to play cards or talk all night?"

"I'm coming," he answered and, turning to me, said, "Try to get some sleep. In the morning you go before the judge. He'll probably let you go." Then he closed the door.

Now I was alone, alone in the darkness, alone with my thoughts, my fears, my humiliation and growing indignation. A small, dirty window up high let in just enough refracted light from a starry, moonlit night to outline walls, the floor, the door and a bunk. I was too upset to lie down and started pacing back and forth like a caged tiger in a zoo. I had always felt so sorry for the animals, locked forever in small cages behind bars. They had done nothing wrong either.

The walls of the cell closed in on me. Only the utmost effort of will and deep breathing kept me from going totally berserk. I knew, if ever I had to choose between a life of imprisonment or death, I would choose death. The worst part of it was the isolation and the total surrender of one's existence. And this was not the rawest prison by far. I thought of Dachau, and other prisons I had heard about. "What made people endure and survive places like that?" I wondered.

Beyond my own anguish, I thought of the panic my parents would be in, not knowing what had happened to me. They, too, would pace the floor all night, house bound, not able to contact anybody.

Exhaustion finally took over. I collapsed on the bunk and fell asleep.

When I opened my eyes again, it was morning. Though I had no watch and no idea what time it was, banging outside in the corridor told me that the prison day had begun.

I sat up and stared at the wall in front of me. Dozens of prisoners before me had etched their initials and comments in it, some in the form of poems. For a little while it kept my mind occupied. With a nail file, I added my initials, including date and year. Suddenly the small, barred window in the door lifted and a female warden shoved a tray with a bowl full of mush and a cup of coffee through the opening. "Get your breakfast," she ordered.

"What time is it?" I asked, taking the tray. Instead of an answer, she slammed the window down again. My stomach felt empty but I was not hungry. The mush and the coffee tasted awful. I left it. About twenty minutes later, she came back to collect the dishes.

"Please, what time is it? When do I get to see the judge?" I asked again. She saw that I had hardly touched the food.

"Ahhh! Maybe that's not good enough for you?" she needled, again ignoring my questions. She sounded hard as steel and could care less.

"You can have that pig slop," I spouted off.

"You get used to it," she said and slammed the window down again.

Anger now started to override all other emotions. It gave me strength. I took out my hand mirror, and with my tear-soaked handkerchief wiped the smeared mascara off my face, combed my hair and brushed the wrinkles from my clothes. "I'll be ready for that judge,"

I primed myself. "I'm going to give him a piece of my mind." I started to rehearse all the things I was going to say to him.

It was a long wait until the cell door opened and the warden—another woman, built like a tank—escorted me to the cellar where the judge held court. Oh my, what a pitiful sight! Long lines of people cued up in front of an arched, open doorway, many in slippers and nightwear, the old and the young, women on one side, old men on the other. In the room beyond, I saw an American officer sitting behind a large desk, meting out 'justice'. Many women wept, prayed, or just wrung their hands. Men stood stiffly, with twitching faces, staring straight ahead or at the floor.

One by one, the people had to walk up to the judge's desk and answer to charges through an interpreter. The judge, an Ami major, barely looked up from his papers. When he did, he did so with cold indifference bordering on contempt, cutting pleas and explanations short. The meek received papers to sign for their release. Those protesting their arrest landed back in a cell.

Most of the defendants had similar stories. MPs had arrested them at their front door, or as they ran to a neighbor for help, or simply answered the door where an MP stood waiting to haul them away. Many left behind frightened children or a sick family member. Listening to their pathetic stories, seeing their anguish, tore at my heart, but not at the judge's. His total lack of human empathy made me angry. Later I learned that MPs got points for every arrest they made, points that made them eligible for a weekend pass, or even a furlough to the States.

At that moment in time, I did not draw comparisons to the millions the Gestapo had whisked away and off to prisons, to prisons where the only way to freedom and release often was death, and death alone. However, I did expect more justice from those that claimed to have fought against injustice.

A long line of women was still ahead of me when my agent suddenly appeared. The worried wife of one of the musicians had contacted him and reported her husband missing. In turn, the agent checked with the commander of the base where we performed, and when the story of our arrest came to light, he set wheels in motion to get us out. The musicians had already been released. When it was my turn to step up to the desk, my anger boiled over.

"Is that what you call liberation? Is that what you call justice?" I sputtered in messed up English, in a voice saturated with emotion. I doubt if I made any sense at all. My agent stepped hard on my foot, and through his teeth hissed, "Shut up, for God's sake," then bowed and apologized to the judge who shuffled papers, not even bothering to look up.

Unbent and defiant, I walked out of that jail, hoping my jailers could read my thoughts. "You can jail me, but you can't break me." I vowed to take this matter up with the general, if and when I would see him again.

Thinking back on it now, I am surprised I was let go.

Chapter 5

The Birth of La Argentina

$\mathfrak{E}$fforts to clean up Munich intensified. Men, women and children formed bucket brigades to clear away rubble. What they could not reuse, they hauled away in handcarts to dump into tunnels once meant to become Munich's underground rail system.

On days when I did not have to dance, my parents and I went to the woods to gather pine cones, fallen trees and branches in preparation for the cold weather ahead. Our neighbors, the Klohs, owned a garden patch somewhere and raised vegetables. Occasionally, we traded them American canned goods for fresh greens. It helped ease the tension between them and us. My mother and I preserved green beans by stuffing them raw into empty beer bottles with rubber-seal tops, and filling them with water. They kept that way all winter. We also made several trips to the country to barter for eggs, which we put into stone crocks and covered with a kind of gel.

Our American friends, Bob and Harry, had left for home. It was entirely up to me now, to keep our family afloat. My father had no job, no income. Many jobs had collapsed at the end of the war. Though money had no value anymore, we still needed it to pay rent, utilities, and for allotted food rations. Thus far, I had done quite well and turned whatever I earned in money and goods over to my mother. When, on occasion, I asked for a little back to share with a friend, or a person who had done me a favor, Mama became upset and we got into terrible arguments. "Other people always mean more to you than your mother," was her favorite phrase. Sure, we did not have anything in excess, but Frau Klara and the music teacher, who had helped me so much, had even less. Without fail, my mother would pick a fight with them, accusing them of exploiting me. Any other time, my mother was generous to a fault, as long as she could be the giver. "Don't I have any rights? After all, it's I who earned it," I argued. She took it as if I tried to throw it into her face that I supported the family. This caused such a row that I often dreaded to come home.

I noticed that such episodes occurred with almost predictable regularity, every three to four weeks and did as my father did—avoid any confrontations at that time.

That fall, I heard that an old artist's organization had started up again. It met once a week in a bombed-out restaurant in downtown Munich. I went to check it out and met people I knew from long ago. It was there that I learned about a Hollywood producer holding auditions for a big, international road show, to travel all over Europe, to wherever American troops were stationed. The pay would be in American dollars, including American food and lodging. It had everybody excited. Auditions were to be held in Passau, about sixty miles east of Munich. In spite of the difficulties getting there, many decided to try out. So did I.

Having only a little over a week to get ready, I practiced every day to perfect my dance numbers, and saw to it that my costumes were in the best condition possible. The auditions were to last three days and, if needed, overnight accommodations were provided. Nothing of this was in writing, only by word of mouth.

The day the auditions were supposed to begin, I took an early train to Passau, carrying a large suitcase with my costumes and a small rucksack with my lunch and supper. The few trains that ran at the time were so crowded that it was a fight to get on. I finally did, but had to stand up for most of the trip. Passau was the last stop where everyone had to get off. I followed the crowd out of the depot, wondering how far it was to the theater where the auditions were being held. My suitcase was heavy. In front of the station, I saw people load their baggage onto a waiting one-horse cart, then hop on themselves. The driver, I found out, ran a taxi service, letting those who could pay in cigarettes get on first. All others had to walk or wait until he came back. Luckily, I had some cigarettes with me. I shared the ride with a few musicians with large instruments, who had come for the auditions, also.

Upon arrival at the theater, we had to put our name and a description of our act on a list that was already several pages long. "It will be at least a couple of hours before we call you," I was told. Around the outside of the theater, jugglers juggled, acrobats tumbled, musicians tuned their instruments and singers warmed up their vocal cords. It had a sort of carnival atmosphere. Other performers spilled into the dark theater. A few rows from the stage sat three uniformed Americans, leaning back with their feet up on the seat in front of them, shouting directions. A couple of civilians acted as translators. I ate my lunch and watched for a while as they called performers out on the dimly lit stage, one after another. Most of them had barely started when one of the Amis clapped his hands and shouted, "Thank you." That meant he or she was done and had to leave the stage.

The longer I watched, the more nervous I became, especially after several excellent, beautifully costumed classical dancers were called off less than half way through their number. "I won't stand a chance," I told myself. Then a tiny female, bare-footed, draped in flowing layers of lavender-pink fabric, her jet-black hair piled and sculpted on top of her head, appeared on stage and struck a seductive pose on the floor. Her dance, the announcer translated, was an interpretation of Salome and Her Seven Veils. To music with a Near-Eastern flavor, played on a gramophone, she moved gracefully about the stage, shedding one veil after another. She ended her dance by raising the last veil triumphantly above her head, standing bare naked, with just a glittered g-string and glittered pasties on her breasts. Though she was not a well-trained dancer, she was beautiful and a pleasure to watch. One of the men rose from his seat, walked up to the footlights and talked to her. A woman emerged from the wings and draped a robe around the dancer, who then joined the Americans in the audience. No doubt, she was in.

Suddenly, I had serious doubts whether I should even try out, but decided, "Well, I'm here. I might as well go on."

Behind the stage, in the dressing rooms and in the wings, I had trouble finding a space, much less privacy to change into my costume. Among the people around me, I recognized some by name. Not long ago, they had been the stars of the stage, outstanding artists, highly revered by the theater-going German public; now they had to grovel with the rest of us to survive. From day to day I learned more of the meaning of defeat.

In my travels during the war through German-occupied countries, I did not realize what psychological effect it had on people to be under the thumb of a foreign power. I had no way to look into their souls or feel the humiliation as they were being stripped of culture and pride to a point where their souls starved more than their bodies did. Finding myself in their shoes now, I began to understand.

It finally was my turn to go on. For my first number I chose my Spanish dance to music from the gramophone. At this point, I no longer cared to impress the Hollywood producers and did not, like most others, come out and humbly bow to them. Instead, I waited in the wings until the music started, then came out dancing. The exciting part of a Spanish dance is in the controlled passion, always at the edge of exploding. In a good dancer, this passion, regardless of what emotions drive it, sparks through every movement, and sharpens the footwork and the snap of the castanets. My defiance and anger often served me well.

To my surprise, I was allowed to finish. I bowed and walked off stage, but was called back. "They liked your dance," the interpreter said, "but you have too much on. Do you have another costume, something more...more revealing?"

Totally perplexed over the American's taste in the arts and their craving to see flesh, I shook my head and answered flatly, "No. But if that's what it takes, I will have."

"Thank you." I was dismissed.

Artists back stage supported one another with complements, and by making jokes, such as, "Next time I audition in my underwear...no...better make it a G-string."

I decided to take an evening train back home. Waiting for the horse cart to stop by to take some of us back to the station, I met Salome, accompanied by her mother, soaking up the late afternoon sun in a small adjacent park. She was tiny and even more beautiful close up, like a work of art in an exotic sort of way. She would not need to do much to be a sensation, I thought. We exchanged a few words under the watchful eye of her mother, who seemed to be extremely protective of her. "What did you find out about the show?" I asked her.

"The producer has not decided anything yet. He did not find enough material for the kind of show he has in mind. He wants something colorful, fast moving, sexy and funny," she answered.

Suddenly, a light turned on in my head. I knew what I had to do.

That same night, after I came home, I reopened my mother's old trunk and rummaged once again through its musty contents for odds and ends that I could combine into a costume. This time I would not need much material. One of my grandmother's dresses had a broad band of black, beaded tulle with a circular motive at the bottom. I held it across my bosom, stepped in front of the hall mirror, grinned and nodded, "Perfect." Next I found two black ostrich feathers. "Perfect." I also had some black material left over from the Nazi flag, and a white silk skirt from my first formal when I was fourteen.

Next day, I went to see my seamstress, Frau Klara, and showed her the sketch I had made for a costume and the material I wanted to use. When she saw it, she roared.

"I think I've been beating my head against a wall," I told her. "The Amis don't care how intricate and precise my footwork is, or how many pirouettes I can turn. What they want to see is flesh. So, flesh they shall have. It's a lot easier to come by than a good routine."

Frau Klara went immediately to work. She cut off the beaded band, asked me to take off my blouse, and positioned it over my bra. She fitted the beaded circular design with a large bead in its center over my breast. We thought it looked outrageously naughty and started to laugh.

"Perfect," I said. "Let's make this into a bra."

"Are you sure? That's kind of daring, isn't it?

"Damn right. This is my protest dress."

There was just enough left of this material for a hip-hugging band, to which I wanted the skirt attached, half way around the back, leaving my legs exposed in front. Because the skirt was circular, I could pick it up and wrap it around the front, if I wanted to. We played around with it for a little while. By the time I left, she was still laughing and shaking her head.

These were times when a modest two-piece bathing suit was still considered indecent. My costume was even more immodest

Two days later, I came for a fitting. Frau Klara had the entire costume already basted together. We decided to add a narrow lace ruffle around the bra, and cut big flower patterns from the black swastika material to be appliquéd onto the skirt.

"What do you want me to do with the feathers?" she wondered.

I stood in front of her mirror. To me, the whole idea was a farce. In that frame of mind, I stuck the feathers into the deep V front of my beaded hip-band, partially hiding my navel.

"There, how does that look?"

"Are you sure?" Frau Klara looked at me, drawing her brows together.

"Shamelessly brazen, wouldn't you say?"

Again, she shook her head and we laughed and laughed.

It was not long before I got to try out my new costume. I chose to dance a tango in it, aloof and seductively elegant, choreographed to tease, using the skirt in a way to reveal actually very little. I wore it for the first time at another audition for a new agent at the '*Haus der Kunst*' (an art museum in Munich). The agent, Mr. Barretti, had seen me dance before, had given me his card, and invited me to try out for an extravaganza he was asked to put on for General Eisenhower, which was to take place at the museum. He had already seen my Spanish number and asked me what else I had. I smirked and said, "I have a new number, a tango." He asked to see it.

I was a little nervous. Every performer there was so by special invitation only. Well, I thought, I have to test the waters sooner or later. After I finished the tango in my new costume, Mr. Barretti asked me to wait until the audition was over. He wanted to talk to me.

When we met up, one of the first things he said to me was, "We have to change your name. I think we call you *La Argentina*." Next, he informed me that I would perform the tango at the extravaganza for General Eisenhower, and handed me a contract to sign, offering me twice the salary as my other agent. I was dumbfounded.

From then on, I became one of the hottest items on the entertainment circuit.

Protest dress.

Dancing for Americans.

CLOAK AND DAGGER CLUB

MUNICH
MAUERKIRCHERSTR. 75

PROGRAM

We present to-night:

GERDA SOMMERSCHUH	Singer State Opera Munich
FRANZ KLARWEIN	Singer State Opera Munich
NICA SANFTLEBEN	Dancer Opera Ballett Munich
MIMI THOMA	Chansons Cabarett Popp Munich
ELFI LARSEN	Dancer Cabarett Popp Munich
ILONKA-SEWALD	Dance and Arcordeaon, Wintergarden Berlin
KARL WALTER POPP	Master of Ceremonies Munich
HENRY FEHRS	Pianist
JIMMY ARCHER	and his Swing Band plays for Dance

Saturday, May 18th

Mitzi (Elfi Larsen - stage name) 1946.

Chapter 6

Standing Ground

The show for General Eisenhower went well. The enormous lecture hall at the *Haus der Kunst* was packed. Security was tight. Guards posted outside our dressing rooms accompanied us down the risers to the floor where we performed, then back again. They were not allowed to talk to us, but did point out, when asked, where the general sat. However, all we saw of him was his shiny bald head.

Bookings with my new agent took the shows farther and farther away from Munich, to Heidelberg and to Wiesbaden. That meant staying overnight in miserable accommodations—unheated buildings with out-of-order plumbing, musty rooms with shot-out windows, army cots or beds with lumpy, soiled mattresses and linens. The few buildings left intact after the bombings had been claimed by the American army for its use. It was a dog's life. When a contract offer came along from Cabaret Popp, the first and only live theater in Munich that opened after the war, I seriously considered it. An incident at a US air base in Erding near Munich later convinced me to sign.

It was not unusual after a performance that our cast was invited to a small, private gathering at officers' quarters, where we usually were served something to eat and drink. On this particular evening, the women in our cast were asked by some officers from the base to help them set up. We were glad to oblige.

While our show paraphernalia was being loaded onto the truck that was to take us home later, some of us left ahead of the rest in the officers' jeeps. I rode with a captain. After a wild ride across a dark field, he stopped in front of a building, led me inside, and showed me into a large dining room where beer bottles, dirty ashtrays, newspapers and magazines cluttered a huge table.

"Well, so what can I do?" I asked. "Looks like we need to do a little cleaning up."

"Oh, let's just wait until the others get here," he answered.

He went out into the hall, knocking on doors. Nobody else seemed to be in the building.

As the minutes ticked away and nobody showed up, I became increasingly uncomfortable. My sixth sense sounded an alarm. I went out into the hall, looking for the captain.

"Hello! Where are you?"

Down the hall, he stuck his head out of a door. "Come here. Come on in," he urged.

I walked up to him, but stopped at the door of what seemed to be his room. "It doesn't look like anybody is coming. I would appreciate if you'd take me back to the clubhouse. Don't want the truck to take off without me," I said to him.

"I am going to check on that right now. Why don't you wait in here where it's warm? I'll be right back," he tried to reassure me.

"Please, let me come with you. I don't want to stay here all by myself."

"No...no. I'll be right back. Make yourself comfortable," he said and slipped past me and out of the building. Seconds later, I heard his jeep race off.

Still standing in the doorway, I wondered what I should do. At a glance, all I saw of his room was a bed and next to it a night table with a holstered revolver on it. Bed...gun...! A combination that pushed my panic button. I ran down that hallway and out the front door. It was pitch dark outside. The air base was immense and I had no idea where I was or where to go. If caught wandering around a military installation, I could be shot. I did not know what to do. Germans were fair game at the time, subject to the wiles of any individual of the occupying forces. In courts run by Americans, it was their word against ours. And while I found most Americans to be decent, even generous and kind, they did have their share of opportunists and hooligans.

I stood outside the door of the building, freezing, afraid to go out, and afraid to stay in, mulling over my options. By now I had learned to live by my wits. Not quite smart enough to anticipate bad situations but, thus far, I had been creative enough to get out of them.

Cold through and through, I went back inside. The captain's room, at least, was heated. After a half-hour or more, he returned.

"Where are the others? Did you find them?" I asked.

"They have left."

"They have left...? In the truck...?" My stomach knotted.

"Yep."

79

"I thought they were coming over here? What happened?" I was getting frantic.

The captain only shrugged his shoulder as if saying, "What do I care?"

"I've got to get home. How am I supposed to get home?"

"Guess you're stuck with me for the night," the captain said, grinning. "If you are nice to me, I'll take you home tomorrow morning."

He approached me, grabbed hold of my arm and tried to pull me down onto his bed.

"No, no! Please, this is not funny. I have to go home. NOW!" I freed myself and backed away.

"I no longer have a jeep. I had to turn it in," he said matter-of-factly.

At that point, I heard men enter the building, laughing, swearing and slamming things around. The captain locked the door, then casually started to undress.

"You planned this, didn't you? But you won't get away with it. You had better take me home right now or I'll raise hell."

He laughed.

"I'll scream so that the whole base can hear me," I threatened.

"Go right ahead, scream. If that drunken bunch out there hears you, they are going to have a real good time with you." He had a point.

"I'll report you to your commander."

Still laughing, he had stripped down to his shorts.

My heart raced; my mind spun in panic. "Oh, God," I thought, "help me get out of this one."

I forced myself to stay calm, at least outwardly, and studied the man. How could I get to him? What approach should I take? How could I win his sympathy or compassion? Tall, broad shouldered and muscular, with fawn-colored hair and mustache, blue eyes and a square chin, I judged him to be about thirty years of age. He could be married, have a wife and kids, or a sister. Looking around the room, I saw a couple of photos on a small table by the windows. I went to pick one up. It was of a woman with two small children. "Your wife? Your children?" I asked, looking at him, hoping to stir some feelings in him. He jerked the picture out of my hand and put it back on the table, face down.

"I'm going to bed," he said. "What are you going to do? Stand there all night?"

"Tell me about them. How long has it been since you've seen them?" I persisted. As hard as I tried to hide my panic and anger, my voice quivered with it.

He did not answer. The smirk on his face told me that he knew what I was trying to do. He sat down on his bed, reached for the revolver, pulled it out of the holster and checked it out.

"Here," he said, offering me the gun, "if you are so scared, here, take my gun.

"Oh, no!" I shrunk away. I was not going to fall into this trap. As a German, caught with a GI's gun in my hand...oh, I could already hear prison doors slam on my life.

Hands behind his head, the captain stretched out on his bed. "Well, this is going to be a long night for you...but if you should change your mind...?"

What can I do? What can I do? By now it must have been past midnight. My head and body reeled from exhaustion. I ached to sit down and close my eyes but was afraid to.

"You wouldn't have an aspirin, would you? I have a terrible headache. It's making me sick to my stomach," I tried another approach.

"Oh, for Christ's sake," he said, irritated.

"Please. That's not too much to ask, is it?"

Reluctantly he got up, fumbled through his jacket pockets, producing a small bottle of aspirin. "Here." He tossed it to me.

"I can't swallow it without having something to drink. Could you get me some water, please?"

I was trying his patience, I could tell. Cursing under his breath, he unlocked the door and went outside. That was the opportunity I had been waiting for. I shut the door behind him and locked it.

"Hey...hey, what the hell..." he yelled and banged on it. "Open up, or I'll break it down and over your head."

I did not answer.

"I'll call the MP."

"OK, call them. They'll enjoy a good laugh. See if you can explain how I got here, and why and how you got locked out."

He answered with a barrage of curses, insults and threats, and repeatedly threw himself against the door so hard, I was afraid it might give way. I made ready to climb out of a window. Angry male voices yelled at him to shut up. Finally, he left. Everything was quiet. I heard only my pounding heart. I sat down on the edge of his bed, listening, wondering what he would do next. I sat there for a long time, frozen, nerves and muscles tensed to their limit until exhaustion overwhelmed me and I could stay awake no longer. With my feet still on the floor, my body tipped over sideways onto the bed and I fell asleep.

Voices and laughter out in the hall woke me up. It was barely turning light outside. I listened and waited until all was quiet again, then cautiously opened the door and peeked out. When I saw no one in the hall, I ran out. With a determined stride, I headed across the airfield toward a group of buildings and asked the first person I saw, a GI, for directions to the commander's office. He stared at me, confused, as if to say, "What's she doing here?" but pointed toward some buildings. I caused a similar reaction from a clerk at the commander's office, who promptly announced me to him. The commander, a clean-shaven man in his forties, sat behind a large desk. I told him who I was and he remembered me from the show. He was courteous. With tears running down my face, I told him what had happened.

"Do you know the captain's name?" he asked.

I shook my head, "No."

"Can you describe him?"

That, I could.

The commander nodded in recognition. "I'll see that he takes you home," he said. He called his clerk to fetch the captain and told me to have a seat. Though I appreciated the commander's kindness, I wished he would have chosen anyone but the captain to take me home.

I did not have to wait long. An open jeep drove up with the captain in the front seat next to the driver.

"Take her home," the commander ordered sharply, adding, "and let her sit in front." I thanked him.

It was unclear to me why the captain had to come along. That was definitely not his choice. Without giving me a glance, he badgered the driver to hurry it up.

A light drizzle that morning turned to snow, the first snowfall of the season, and quite unexpected. The large windshield protected me from the freezing wind and driving sleet. I was grateful to the commander for having me sit in the front. In the broad rearview mirror, I could watch the captain in the back slouching further and further down in his seat, tightening his hood. Snow and ice crusted his mustache and eyebrows, and collected in the crevices of his jacket around the collar and the edge of his hood.

As we came into Munich, driving down *Ludwigstrasse* toward the *Odeonsplatz*, the driver asked for directions to my house.

"Don't bother," the captain yelled at him over the roar of the engine. "Stop the car." The driver pulled over to the side of the street. "You," the captain pointed at me, "get the hell out...get out! You can find your own way home from here."

For a moment, the driver hesitated, clearly embarrassed. He looked at me, shrugged his shoulders as if apologizing, "Sorry. There is nothing I can do. He outranks me."

Before I got out, I turned and looked squarely into the captain's frozen, frosted face and grinned with spiteful glee. Should his nose have fallen off from frostbite, it would have been what he deserved. It was nothing more than justice the commander had so wisely meted out.

No sooner did my feet touch the sidewalk, the captain had hoisted himself into the front seat and ordered the driver to "Let's go! Let's get the hell back to the base."

I took a streetcar home.

"My God, where have you been? We were beside ourselves with worry," my parents greeted me as I walked in.

That cinched it. The very next day, I signed on with Cabaret Popp.

Chapter 7

Trials

Cabaret Popp had become a Mecca for German artists, poets, composers and playwrights, many already
well-known, others whose star was rising. Performing there, and to be accepted by them, would give my
wilting confidence as a dancer a much needed boost.
I shared the stage with big names like Mimi Thoma, a
popular singer, and Eugen Roth, a witty poet who sati-
rized the human condition.

I was very nervous on opening night, knowing that
the audience would judge me on my ability to perform,
not on how much skin I bared. When Herr Popp came
back stage after the show, shaking my hand and con-
gratulating me, "You were a hit, girl," my insides turned
summersaults. I had passed the test. "They liked
me...they liked me!" I felt like shouting it from the highest mountaintop. And what a relief it was not to hear
anybody yell "Take it off." This sense of euphoria was
short lived, however.

With the cold, damp weather, the ache and the swelling of my joints returned. Each day began with the painful process of loosening up my body so that by night I could dance again. Aspirin helped some, but that, too, was hard to come by.

Our apartment felt like the inside of a cooler. We could only afford to build a fire in the kitchen stove to cook our meals; even so, the small allotment of coal for the winter had dwindled quickly. So had the stockpile of pinecones and kindling hauled home all summer long from the woods. Homemade briquettes made from newspapers kept the embers glowing and the water in a built-in cistern tepid, but gave off no heat. My mother and I perpetually shivered. This was only the beginning of winter. Having nothing to trade on the black market, the outlook was grim. Every night when I came home my mother lamented that she did not know anymore what to put on the table. She had to stand in line for hours, in pouring rain or blowing snow, just to get an onion, a head of cabbage, a little saccharine, a pound of flour, a cup of sugar, and our monthly rations of margarine and meat, no bigger than the size of an egg. She did that diligently every day, coming home cold and often drenched to her skin to our unheated apartment. While she stood in line in front of one store, my father and I would queue up in front of another, always an hour before it opened and still often came home empty handed.

It soon became painfully clear that, while I enjoyed the artistically stimulating atmosphere at the Cabaret, without the food and cigarettes from the Americans, it was impossible to survive. I simply had to work for them again and had to count myself lucky that I could.

I must say, had it not been for the individual American GIs, many more German families would have starved or frozen to death that winter. Many did.

Against army regulations, I saw GIs hand out leftovers from their mess halls to adults and hungry children who raided their garbage cans. Others adopted a German family as their home away from home. What irony! Only months before, our two sides had killed one another on command. Now, our enemy had turned into our friend, helping us to survive. Such is the absurdity of war.

Most Germans genuinely liked the Amis and even came to admire their relaxed nonconformity and free spirit. People drew comparisons between them and our own troops and started to question if our highly esteemed discipline was really that great of a virtue.

"We are so lucky to be in the American zone," I heard people say everywhere. Indeed. Escapees from the eastern zone told horror stories of Russian troops raping, plundering and—as Nazis did to Jews, Poles and Russians—carting the able-bodied off to labor camps. The British, it was said, were quite proper, but they themselves were starving. Even if they had wanted to help, they had nothing to spare. Besides, it seemed that the British and the French also held more of a grudge against Germans than did the individual American.

The Amis' manners and tastes, however, still took something to get used to. We Germans shook our heads. It would have been unthinkable for a German, or any European official to sit slouched behind his desk with his feet up on it, conducting business. Was this an expression of disrespect? Or did they behave this way in the States also? As we puzzled over the Amis' social customs, they laughed at ours—always shaking hands, bowing, and clicking heels.

Young Germans liked the Amis' music, the jazz and the songs—music that had been banned during the Third Reich, but could be heard now and then at pri-

87

vate gatherings. My friend Hanni often came to my house when we had Amis visiting, asking them to write down the lyrics to the songs. Our favorites were: *Always, Stardust, You are my Sunshine, and My Dreams Are Getting Better All The Time.*

Eventually, people accepted the Amis' tastes and behavior as differences in culture. I drew a line. It remained a scarring, humiliating experience for me every time the Ami's yelled, "Take it off!" I also could not understand why the Amis went wild over somebody with two sticks and a little rhythm, beating the hell out on a drum, but booed and fled en masse at the first few bars of a symphony or opera.

◆　◆　◆

By the fall of 1945, the Nuremberg War-Crimes Trials had shifted into high gear. The proceedings could be heard on the radio and dominated the daily news. Reaction to it by the German public was mixed. Some dismissed it with a wave of the hand. "What can you expect? We lost the war. Had we won, heads would roll on the other side." Others cried foul for trying German generals. Still, others remembered angrily the firebombing of cities like Cologne, Hamburg, Bremen, Dresden and Munich where within minutes tens of thousands of civilians perished in the flames and explosions, mostly woman and children. "That was not a war crime?" people asked.

My father cynically referred to the trial as "the victors' grandstanding finale."

"Why don't they call it what it is? It's a trial of Germany," he said.

"If they really meant to try war crimes, many of the allies would be sitting in the defendants seat also," I reasoned.

88

"Might makes right! That's how it has always been. That's how it still is." My father summarized these events matter-of-factly, like a man who had seen it all before, and who had learned to accept the inevitable.

I happened to listen to one of the broadcasts in which the Allies accused the German army of the Katyn Forest massacre. "What...?" I exploded. "How dare the Allies let those Russians get away with that! They all know that this is an outright lie."

"They won the war," my father said.

From then on, the Nuremberg Trial had lost much of its credibility for me. I considered it as a badly scripted, miscast melodrama. In my eyes, there was not a nation free of guilt.

While on the Russian front entertaining German troops, I gained some insight into political intrigue. I came uncomfortably close to being a co-conspirator against Hitler and the Nazi regime by keeping silent about information entrusted to me. Based on it, I knew that the Western powers could have stopped the war years earlier, perhaps, saving millions of lives on all sides, and sparing millions more the horror of Nazi concentration camps and Siberian prison camps.

It was in the summer of 1943, in a little township deep inside Russia. The German army was in rapid retreat and, hour-by-hour, our chances of escape and survival diminished. While under heavy bombardment by Russian artillery, seeking shelter in an underground bunker, I was privy to a discussion between high-ranking German officers and aristocrats, including the Prince of Prussia. These men, including the Prince, vented their frustration over unsuccessful, secret negotiations with the unyielding Western Allies. Their proposed plan was to stop the war and the killing in Europe, take control of the German army, do away with the Nazi regime, and then, together with the Western forces, go on to eliminate Stalin and his cruel, tyrannical regime as well. As long as he was in power, there would be no peace in Europe. But the Western Allies chose to remain loyal to and honor their pact with the Russian dictator, who was as bad, if not worse than Hitler. They kept insisting on unconditional surrender—terms no army officer, no matter under what flag, could commit his country to and accept.

To this day, my blood runs cold when I think back on that conversation. These men openly talked treason. While I admired them, I was scared to death, for them as well as myself. By listening and not reporting what we had heard, my colleagues and I became coconspirators. I don't know what made them trust us. They put their lives in our hands. Perhaps, because at the time none of us thought we would survive anyway. "One can die only once," the men said. The prince and other royals had already come under suspicion and had been abruptly ordered back to Berlin, fearing the worst.

It seemed futile now to speculate what would have happened, had they succeeded.

But there were also other reasons why I thought the trial hypocritical. How could the Western governments align themselves with Stalin in the first place, endorsing a tyrant no better than Hitler, who murdered millions of his own people? I also could not understand why just about every country in the world, including those presiding at the trial, had closed their borders to, and turned away political and Jewish refugees, sending shiploads back into the hands of their brutal executioners. I had heard Nazi propaganda brag, "No one in the world wants them. Why should we?" Thus justifying the deportation of Jews.

"Justice? Where is justice?" I asked. My father was right. This was not a trial to seek justice. It was the victors' grandstanding. Might makes right.

On the other hand, what particularly angered my father and many other Germans was the conspicuous absence of some of the most hated figures within Hitler's circle—Himmler, Eichman, Bormann, just to name a few. "Cowards," people referred to them. Himmler and Bormann, it was said, committed suicide; others were in hiding or had fled the country. They belonged on the stand next to Goebbles and Hitler. Many Germans wanted to see them tried and hanged. There were, however, still those, women in particular, who were not convinced that Hitler had a hand in the concentration camp murders. They believed that Hitler had been deceived, gone mad, or that he himself was in the clutches of his henchmen. How could a man, who so glorified womanhood and motherhood, be capable of such crimes? They believed in him like others believed in God.

"Look around you. Look where he has led us," my father reminded the doubters, shaking his head. Their dog-like loyalty made him more sad than angry. We knew some of these believers casually. They appeared to be honest, decent, hard working, family-oriented, church-going citizens. There was not one among them who had not suffered losses—family members, friends, their homes. Still, blinded by their faith, like followers of some religious cult, even that could not shake their loyalty and belief in the Fuehrer. They had forfeited to him their power to think and to reason. They had forfeited their minds. "If they can be so misled, what happened here can happen again, anywhere, any time," my father said.

The Nuremberg Trial became a frequent subject of debate. Statisticians argued numbers. When I first heard that three million Jews were put to death in concentration camps, I thought it was an outrageous exaggeration by the Allies, a figure they had plucked out of the air. Since then, the numbers had grown to four millions, then five million. The spotlight suddenly fell on these numbers, taking away from the human aspects—the injustice, the pain and suffering of human beings. My heart could not mourn more for millions than for just one—each one.

The most gruesome images of concentration camp victims appeared repetitiously with any new information on billboards. The pictures showed a multitude of hollow-eyed skeletal corpses being dragged and dumped unceremoniously on top of one another into deep, long ditches. My soul cried out, "God, where are you?" Many of the naked victims seemed to have died only hours before their liberation, all at the same time, hundreds of them. Most women took one look, paled and turned away. Only a few—older men and curious youths—lingered to read the print.

I blinked away tears to read the text. The articles quoted English or American journals, lashing out at us Germans—all Germans—accusing and denouncing us as warmongers, barbarians and willing partners in these crimes. As if the sun had suddenly fallen from the sky, I felt a shadow descend, a shadow that was to follow me for much of my life.

I looked up at my father, who stared at these pictures and the text, flexing his jaw muscles. "The English broadcasts never mentioned anything about this," he muttered. "Did they, or did they not know about it? Surely, they knew more than we did. Why did they keep this quiet?" My father turned away. His face had grayed.

Once the initial shock wore off, I pondered the question, "If we had been told about this, would that have changed anything? Would we have believed it? What could we have done?" Even the victims did not seem to know what fate awaited them, or they would have staged an uprising. It seemed to me that if one faces certain death and has nothing to lose, one would go down fighting. I caught myself assuming. How easy it is to speculate what one would or could have done! For a moment I forgot how paralyzing fear can be, how it can rob one's breath and voice.

From history and experiences my father had shared with me, I knew how extremely cruel some people can be. But for human beings to conceive, much less carry out such a systematic, large scale massacre was beyond mine or anybody else's comprehension.

Had the truth been known...? Only by taking control of the army, as some of our highest German officers sought to do, could this have been prevented. The individual was powerless.

◆ ◆ ◆

From the day the Nazis took over the German government, they squashed with brutal force even the smallest voice of opposition. Secrecy and fear quickly isolated people, thus rendering them ineffectual. Gradually and systematically, the Nazis arrested anyone who did not fit into their ideological slot. First, they targeted opposing political factions to reestablish order in the streets. The public was glad to be rid of these warring gangs. Next, they rounded up known "perverts" and members of certain religious sects. Again, the public was not too empathetic. These arrests happened sporadically, unexpectedly, swiftly and often brutally, before dawn and out of public view. Threats of reprisals silenced witnesses. Moreover, the Nazi regime controlled what teachers taught, newspapers printed, and the radio broadcast. It controlled the church. Anyone who did not conform, who did not submit to their mandates, would lose his job or quietly disappear.

As a young child growing up, I simply mimicked my parents and reacted to the world around me like they did. Along the way, however, I gathered experiences that seemed to support what they were saying. One sunny day, when I was about six or seven years old, I played in the front yard of our apartment building when flag carrying columns of brownshirts came marching down the street. Pedestrians stopped and watched. Suddenly, one marcher, followed by a few others broke rank, jumped on and beat an onlooker to the ground and left him lying in a pool of blood. This happened so quickly, so suddenly, and was over before people had a chance to react. I ran into the house and told my parents, who came out to investigate. It turned out that the man had either improperly saluted or failed entirely to salute the 'blood flag,' the Nazi's most sacred symbol. Some thought that he held up his fist, which was the communist's salute. For weeks afterwards, people talked about this incident in hushed voices, looking right and left and over their shoulders, already in the grip of fear that the wrong person might be listening.

In second grade, I came to school one day and the crucifix above the teacher's desk had been replaced with a picture of Hitler. We did not say our usual prayer to start the day, and were told that from now on we had to stand up and say "Heil Hitler" instead of "Good Morning" or "Good Day" when an adult entered the classroom.

"Heil Hitler" became an official, required salutation. Many stubborn Bavarians stuck to "Gruess Gott" saying, "I'll say 'Heil Hitler' when I see him hanging on the cross."

Around the same time, I had a school friend named Ester. I never saw her father. Finally, I asked her, "Did your father die?" For a long time she evaded my questions, but eventually told me that the Gestapo had taken her father away because he was a Bibleforscher (a Jehovah's Witness). "Please, please, don't say anything to anybody, or they'll take my mother away, too," she implored me.

One morning in 1936, at the crack of dawn, the Gestapo pounded on our door. They wanted to know the whereabouts of a friend of my father's. When he said he did not know, they took him away. His friend, Herr Hilsenbeck, an inventor of sorts, worked on formulas to retrieve precious metals from industrial wastes. At the time, he extracted silver from film developing solutions, then melted it into bars in his wife's oven and sold it. The Nazis got wind of it and demanded that he turn over his formula and the silver to them. He managed to stall them long enough to escape, fleeing only moments before the Gestapo raided his residence. Since my father had worked for him, they came after him. I remember my mother's panic and we feared that we would never see him again. When they let him go a day later, we were surprised and relieved. My father only told us that he had played dumb. Hilsenbeck's neighbors corroborated that he showed up for work as usual, thus could not have known that Hilsenbecks had fled. But from then on, we were under surveillance. Our mail was censored with sections blacked out, especially in the letters my mother received form her sisters in the United States. Much later, we learned that the Hilsenbecks had fled to Italy and lived there under an assumed name. My parents now lived in constant fear. Well-meaning friends urged my father to join the party and to remove himself from suspicion, but he refused.

I also remember the *Kristallnacht* (the night of broken glass). During the night of November 9, 1938, the official, full-scale savagery against the Jews began. In every major city, brownshirts stormed Jewish shops, breaking windows and setting synagogues afire. My parents read about it in the morning paper. "Hoodlums! Bandits!" they called the perpetrators.

Days later, I went shopping with my mother at the popular department store *Horn am Stachus* in Munich. Its big show-windows had been smashed, and the word "*Jude*" had been painted on the walls in big letters. Horn held a 'going out of business' sale and we lined up in front of its doors with many other people, mostly women. Picture-snapping hecklers tried to intimidate us shoppers with anti-Semitic slogans and threats. A brawl ensued as some women fought back. My mother and I looked on, scared, but not budging. The next day, a picture appeared on the front page of the newspaper with us and other shoppers as "people who patronize Jews."

There were public protests, but they were squelched quickly and forcefully, and life went on. For the great majority of Germans who could prove their Arian bloodline, who conformed to the dictates of the Nazi regime, life was good. They prospered. Foreign visitors were impressed by Germany's bloom.

Conformity simply meant joining and paying dues to the Nazi party, keeping one's thoughts to oneself, and greeting public officials with "Heil Hitler" instead of "*Gruess Gott.*" That entitled them to good jobs, new and better housing, free health care, free education for their children, vacations, and many other benefits. The better they lived, the harder it was for them, I assume, to risk it all by rebelling against policies of which they disapproved. And it was not just a matter of economics, but a matter of life and death. It meant risking one's life, and the life of one's family—one's wife, children, mother and father. I wondered if the arm-chair heroes condemning us would have passed the test.

Quiet, stubborn resisters like my father paid the price by being pushed to the bottom of the economic scale. Many others worked quietly and inconspicuously for changes within the ranks, from the highest to the lowest, branded now as Nazis, too, because they had worn the Nazi uniform. Given a choice, this was the course I would have chosen, but I was still too young. These insiders took grave personal chances to help many people and save many lives, but now were being arrested and thrown into jail like criminals. Few of them, if any, had their kind and heroic deeds acknowledged or had their honor restored. To this day, their existence has been mostly ignored by the press.

While the Nuremberg Trials had opened many issues for discussion, they prepared the ground for new hate to sprout. Daily, more findings of Nazi atrocities exploded in blazing, editorials against Germany and Germans on front pages of the foreign press. These articles hammered away at the German population and, of course, bred resentment. It also affected the attitudes of Americans. Germans, already on their knees, their cities in ashes, their homes destroyed, sons, brothers, fathers killed in action or dying in Russian prison camps, quietly shouldered the guilt as a nation, but rejected these personal attacks. It put Germans, including me, on the defensive, prevented open and honest discussions, and finally silenced many of us. It became clear that the world did not want to hear what we had to say.

New arrivals from America gradually replaced the combat troops. Many came already with an attitude, fanned by the American media that all Germans were Nazis. Again and again, I had to defend myself: "No, I did not know about gas chambers in the concentration camps. No, I did not know about the fate of the Jews. No, I did not endorse or support Nazi policies. No, I did not..." It did not matter what I said. Already poisoned by the press, their mind was set. We were all Nazi criminals. They did not question that most of Hitler's victims themselves did not know about gas chambers and the 'final solution,' yet insisted that every German knew.

Angry, I asked, "What did those critics and hindsight experts know about life under a ruthless dictatorship? What did they expect the average German to do? Go to war with broomsticks against machinegun-wielding Nazi thugs?"

I thought of many wealthy, famous and celebrated Jews that had fled Germany early on. They did not stay around to help save their less privileged brothers and sisters. Where was their voice? Of course, they, too, could not have known or guessed what lay in store for Hitler's rejects. But had they known, would they have stayed and fought?

Reading the indicting comments in the papers, I asked, "Have we not been punished enough already for our ignorance and the crimes of our government? Millions dead, our cities in ruin, millions more left homeless and starving. Is that not enough?"

Evidently that was not enough for a self-righteous world and self-appointed, self-righteous judges who fed on this tragedy, trying to elevate themselves by painting the German nation as a nation of murderers. "Germans should never be forgiven...not for generations to come." This was the official message repeated over and over again. Though Hitler and his regime were dead, hate was not. Already consumed by grief and pain, at the brink of existence, these attacks further traumatized the German people.

"How clean are the hands that crack the whip?" some people asked. These issues hung around in people's minds, but seldom aired in their conversations. I felt tension building.

The message I received was that being good or bad did not matter. What mattered was to be on the winning side. This further eroded once strongly held ideals and the hope for a tomorrow and a better world. At the age of nineteen, I was turning into a bitter, disillusioned cynic.

"Next time, I swear, I'm going to say "Heil Hitler," or "Heil Moscow," or "Heil Whatever," I told my father. "There is no justice. Principles don't matter. What you get for them is a slap in the face. On the right side, you can do no wrong; on the wrong side, you can do no right." I felt defeated. "Who cares? The world doesn't, and neither does God."

My father only looked at me as if searching for an answer. His answer never came. I had to find it on my own, and eventually I did.

GIs that helped us survive.

Morris Katz.

Billy the Greek.

Nice fellow.

Capt. Smith.

Mariahilfkirche - Munich,
destroyed 1944.

My teacher Lisa Kresse.

Chapter 8

Christmas 1945

Days inched toward Christmas, the first after the war. I worked again for the Americans for cigarettes and food. We traded part of the cigarettes for coal, and with the rest my father went to the village where he grew up to trade them for whatever he could get—flour, butter, eggs, possibly even a Christmas goose. Mama and I thoroughly cleaned our apartment, then decorated it with boughs of evergreens from the forest. I made a small Advent wreath, attached used red candles saved from prior years, and placed it on top of the radio.

On evenings when I was home, after we ate and did the dishes, we lit the candles, one for each week of Advent. Their soft, dancing light kindled precious memories of peace, warmth and harmony. Papa reached for Mama's hand and, in halting, broken sentences, with a tremor in his voice, he thankfully acknowledged that the war was over, that we still had a roof over our heads, and that we had each other. He paused, his gaze fixed on a picture of his son hanging on the wall above where he usually sat. The silence cut into me like a knife. The loss of Willi and Pepi still throbbed in my chest like an open wound. Mama put her arms around Papa's neck and for long seconds they stood in a tight embrace. We hid our tears from one another, avoiding even to utter Willi's name for fear of breaking to pieces.

A few minutes later, we blew out the candles to make them last, and watched in silence as the thin threads of smoke from the extinguished wicks curled upward, "Like souls rising from bodies of the dead," spreading the scent of melted wax.

Candle wax and pine scent mixed in the air, triggering visions of Christmases past. Sitting around the kitchen table, soaking up the cozy warmth still radiating from the cook stove, my parents rehashed with relish and with special pride the many Christmas programs in which I had performed as a child. It had been the highlight of their lives.

On stage before the age of six, I acted in plays, danced, or recited verses and prologues. Mama was in her absolute glory when people told her afterwards that I had the makings of another Shirley Temple. "If you just would practice a little harder," she used to prod me, "we could be rich. We would not have to beg the milkman, the baker, the butcher and the landlord to let us charge just one more time." When I sometimes rebelled against her constant pushing, she scolded me and told me about her own dreams of being on stage. "I would have given anything if my parents had let me take dancing lessons and go on stage. You don't know how lucky you are."

Of course, Papa beamed just as much. Following each performance he searched through newspapers for reviews, that Mama carefully clipped out and saved. But I was just a child. Constantly practicing, learning new parts, long texts and new dances took up much time, time other children spent at play, and I resented it. Yet, I was aware that had it not been for my performing, I would have missed out on many festive, fun occasions. Now it helped us to survive.

While my parents reminisced about my performances, I craved after the sights, tastes and smells at these festivities. Around Christmas time, every place, every hall where I performed had been transformed into a fairytale world. From ceiling to walls, the room glittered with tinsel-tossed boughs, wreathes and garlands, that filled the air with pine scent. Rows of white-covered tables, decorated with gold and silver ribbons and candles further enhanced the eye appeal. But what attracted me the most was the usual display of gift baskets that would later be raffled off for some good cause. From them emanated such heavenly, mouthwatering scents of oranges, mandarins, apples, and cinnamon *Lebkuchen,* items my family could seldom afford.

I could hardly wait for that part of the program when the candles on huge trees on either side of a stage were lit and musicians finished playing '*Silent Night.*' That was the cue for Saint Nickolaus to make his grand entrance. For me, this was the highlight of the evening. Dressed in white, wearing a gold trimmed robe and bishop's hat, holding a shepherd's staff and followed by angels in long, white tunics with golden wings and halos, Saint Nickolaus stepped upon the stage and addressed the children. From a thick, gold embossed book where he supposedly had kept records about each child's behavior, good and bad, he read off names.

"I see that Hansi did not always pay attention in school," he said, paused, and scanned the audience as if looking for him. "Then there is Karl and Franzl who skipped school. And Willi and Seppi...," he continued. These names, of course, were so common that every other boy in the audience felt addressed personally and slid down in his seat, trying to hide.

"And the girls...there is Maria, Gretchen, Lisl..."

He always ended on a conciliatory note, reminding the children to be good and to mind their parents. Then, with the help of his angels, he handed out a bag full of goodies to each child, filled with fruit, nuts, cookies and candies.

Remembering these times was sweet torture. It stirred cravings that could not be satisfied, maybe for a long time to come.

At functions put on by the '*Winter Hilfe,*' a government sponsored winter aid program, the gift packages also contained toys and things to wear. These had been such happy times for my family, even under Hitler's thumbscrew.

Signs of the season appeared on American bases also. Most places where I performed had a Christmas tree with electric lights and some of the oddest ornaments, from socks to auto parts. Our shows often were part of a unit's Christmas party, and there I encountered for the first time an American Santa in his red, white trimmed suit, white beard, and stuffed belly. The Amis seemed in a celebratory, jolly mood, especially the fighting units, who looked forward to going home.

As more and more replacements arrived from the US, that included many American women in uniform, I noticed a change, a cooling off. Audiences no longer seemed as boisterous, and clubs not quite as generous. Many 'Off Limits' signs appeared to keep Germans out. Previously, members of the show received a hot meal either before or after their performance. Now, we were lucky to get a sandwich. We were no longer welcomed into mess halls and some clubs, except as someone's special guest. Even then, we frequently encountered hostility. "What is this *Kraut* doing in here? Get these *Krauts* out of here."

"Why don't they just put up signs, 'Dogs and Germans not allowed?' one of my colleagues growled. In the eyes of some we were no longer people, or Germans; we were simply '*Krauts*' (cabbages) now. It was not morally challenging to kick a cabbage around.

Audiences where American women were present refrained from yelling, "Take it off!" Instead, they pressured club managers who in turn pressured our agent to have one of us females perform topless, threatening to deny us payment and transportation home if we should refuse. Agent Baretti successfully negotiated us out of most such situations, letting it be known that he had friends in high places who would not approve. The few times he did not succeed, we females had to draw straws. We cried. We begged. A club manager sometimes upped the ante by throwing an extra carton of cigarettes into the deal. "Take it or leave it," he would say, reminding us how lucky we were that he was an American and not a Nazi German. Suddenly, the fate of every member of the show fell on a few of us women.

One time, a male member of our cast challenged a club manager, "What do you do if we all simply refuse to do the show? You can throw us out on the street, but how do you save your face?"

"That's how," the manager answered, drew his pistol and ordered the man outside. That threw us into a state of panic. Baretti pleaded, "We'll do the show. We'll do the show. Just let him go."

We women drew straws. One time I drew the short end. All the heat from my body seemed to rush into my cheeks while the rest of me started to shiver and shake. I had to sit down. My legs buckled and threatened to collapse underneath me. Beseechingly and eyes wide with fear, my colleagues stared at me, waiting for what I might say or do. Baretti squirmed and tried a few more times to persuade the manager to abandon his request.

A singer, Irmgard, about my age; Rosi, a dancer and acrobat, a few years younger than myself; and a young, pretty juggler's assistant were the only other women in the show. "It's me, or one of them. I drew the lot." I wanted to squirm out of it, but when I looked into the terrified faces, especially Rosi's, I could not.

"You can make it a short number and we can dim the lights," Baretti suggested in a low, calm tone of voice, "but you must do it...for everybody's sake...you must. This guy hates Germans. No telling what he might do."

Thoughts whirled through my mind so fast they made no sense. Rosi's face was white as the wall she leaned against. Images surfaced, of her and myself as children in dance school together. I still saw that shy and timid little girl in her. Almost eighteen now, she had not changed much.

I took a deep breath, clenched my teeth and rose to my feet, suddenly reenergized. "Tell that brute," I said to Baretti, "I am upping the ante. It'll cost him two cartons of cigarettes...and I want them now. I won't change into any costumes until then." I figured this brute had a lot at stake, also. He could rough up a man or two, but he still needed a show that night to save his face.

Baretti looked at me as if I had lost my mind, but related my message. A short while later he came back, grinning, and handed me two cartons of cigarettes. I threw them into my suitcase. This was not about cigarettes. I wanted to let this jerk of a manager know he could not just walk over us.

"My...with that, you can almost buy a house," the juggler's assistant remarked, suddenly having second thoughts, perhaps, why she did not make that deal herself.

I instructed the musicians to cut the coda, which shortened my number significantly. When it was my turn, I strode out onto the show floor, defiant, head held high, covering myself with one end of my long, silken skirt, holding the other end extended to the back. During my dance I switched between one and the other, a technique I once saw a fan-dancer use. This way I stayed covered, except for the split seconds when I changed. I finished with both arms crossed in front, bowed, then waited for the applause to die and said, "I want you all to know that I was forced to do this," then walked off with as much dignity as I could muster. My mouth was so dry that my lips stuck to my teeth. Behind me, I heard murmurs ripple through the crowd.

Back in the dressing room I broke into sobs. Rosi put her arms around me and cried with me. Hers were tears of relief.

It is hard to describe the shame and humiliation I felt, and then the terror deep inside before every new show. "What will they ask of us this time? What will they do to us?" We were at the mercy of any bully that came along and we had no recourse. Such incidents were few, depending only on what kind of person was in charge, but the fear was always present. When sometimes hurt and anger flared, it did not last because the majority of Americans we had met, like people everywhere, were more than decent, and a few stood out like beacons of light, healing my hurt, dissolving my anger, and renewing my faith in the human race.

◆　◆　◆

It was Christmas Eve. In the morning, Mama and I decorated a small spruce tree Papa had brought home on his bike from an outdoor market in downtown Munich. In the afternoon I delivered a few little 'thank you' packages bound in small fabric remnants containing tiny portions of instant coffee, a few cigarettes, chewing gum and much needed items like matches or cigarette lighters that had been given to me by GIs. Still hidden away, I had a pair of fur-lined slippers for Mama, and Ami earmuffs and a new coffee mug for my father, all bought on the black market. Two days before, Papa had gotten the goose, which Mama and I had plucked and dressed, and given to the butcher to store until Christmas day.

I tried hard to recapture a little of the magic Christmas had held for me as a child, but missing were all the sights and sounds. Though we never had much money to buy anything, we used to go downtown just to look at all the brightly lit store displays with enchanting, animated snow villages, with dolls and sleds and toys galore. Vendors at busy street corners sold freshly roasted chestnuts out of drum ovens, sending off irresistible aromas. A small bag full only cost ten Pfennig, and warmed our hands as well as our stomachs.

Even more enticing to the senses was the *Kristkindlmarkt*, where merchants set up acres of booths outdoors, offering all sorts of temptations for the palate and the eye—from candy garlands, Lebkuchen hearts, to grilled sausages; gadgets, clothes, pottery and jewelry. Musicians and carolers added a festive touch, and often heaven contributed to the wonder with gently falling snow, transforming the scene into a shimmering fantasy. For a child, this was pure magic. Now, all of it was gone. Nothing downtown reminded me of Christmas, only of terror and death. Even the radio replayed mostly the horror of the recent past. I cried when I thought of it. Another layer of my childhood had been stripped from me.

Around the holidays, I felt a strong urge to attend church again, remembering what a festive, elevating experience high mass used to be, especially in one of the many magnificent cathedrals that had graced the city. That, too, was not the same anymore. The houses of God had crumbled under the fury of war like any other building. So had my faith. I no longer believed in what had been preached within, but I still clung to the church-inspired traditions.

On Christmas Eve, after a simple evening meal, we lit the few, small candles clipped to the branches of the tree and exchanged gifts. Mama had crocheted a bed jacket for me out of bits and pieces of reclaimed yarn, hoping it would soothe my aching joints. Papa surprised me with a rabbit's foot. Not only was it a symbol of good luck, its soft fur made the best powder puff. Mama was thrilled over the slippers and wore them immediately. Papa appreciated the earmuffs, but thought that his old chipped coffee mug was still good enough for him.

On this the holiest of nights, the air used to vibrate with the sound of countless church bells from near and far. People came out of their homes to listen. The radio played Handel and Bach, and featured children's choirs singing Christmas carols. One of my favorite carols was *"Hohe Nacht der klaren Sterne."* Unfortunately, it always came just before Propaganda Minister Goebbels delivered his annual Christmas speech. Maybe because of that connection, I have never heard it played again. Certain music, including Wagner, had been banned after the war for reasons we could not understand.

The instant Goebbels came on, Mama's hands went up to cover her ears. "Turn him off. I can't stand to

listen to that liar," she would say. Papa grudgingly complied. He liked to stay informed, always reading between the lines. For him it was like a weather forecast
that indicated possible changes in the climate and he
wanted to track the storm.

For six years we had carried on with the Christmas
traditions under the shadow of war, holding on to
memories of happier times. For some, this was all they
had left...memories. While we lit candles, eternal darkness descended for so many others.

Christmas Day. We got up early to prepare our mid-
day feast of roast goose, potato dumplings, and cabbage salad. Papa's job was grating the raw potatoes
and squeezing them dry. Mama put the feet, wings,
head, neck and giblets of the goose into a brine of salt
and vinegar for a traditional New Year's dinner, called
Gaenseklein.

Finally, the goose was in the oven, the water for
the dumplings was heating on top of the stove, the salad
was made, and we could clean up the mess we had
made in the kitchen.

I set the table, spreading our best linen tablecloth
that Mama and I had embroidered over the everyday
worn and frayed oil cloth, placed the odds and ends of
plates and tableware on it, and added a few twigs of
spruce for decoration. "Someday," I dreamed out loud,
"I'm going to have a nice set of matching dishes and
silverware."

Mama, in the meantime, carefully skimmed the
goose fat off the juices in the roasting pan to use later
for cooking or to spread on bread. At last, dinner was
on the table. My mouth already watered. However,
the mere sight of all this good food overwhelmed us
with emotions. We hesitated to take the first bite.

"How lucky we are," Papa said. He turned away,
took out his handkerchief and blew his nose. We knew

that millions that day did not have a home, a fire to warm them, or a meal to sustain them. I felt guilty to be so rich.

That evening, I had to perform at an air base near Munich. After the show, an American band played dance music. We were invited to stay and I learned to dance the swing and jitterbug. I sat with a bunch of nice fellows and had a good time. One, called Morris, was the cook at the base. In his late twenties, tall and a little on the pudgy side, he had a jolly good nature that put me at ease. Having only a few short months left in the service, he celebrated and looked forward to going home.

"Do you know anybody from whom I could buy some nice jewelry to take home with me?" he asked me during the course of our conversation.

As a cook, he had access to food—sugar, butter, oil and coffee—which traded well on the black market. I told him that I knew of a black market dealer in the neighborhood where I lived, with whom my family had traded once or twice. Before I had to leave, he asked if I could connect him with this person, and if he could visit me. Morris was a likable guy, not pushy or fresh, and made no advances. "Sure," I said and gave him my address.

Morris did not waste any time and came to see me the next afternoon. He wore a long, loose army coat. After I introduced him to my parents, who invited him to take off his coat and stay a while, he emptied his pockets—a can of jam, fruit, powdered milk and 'instant' coffee and peanut butter.

"Peanut butter! I could live on peanut butter," I exclaimed. It was one of the things Americans introduced me to and became my favorite food.

Morris placed everything on the table. "Just a little Christmas present for you all," he said.

"Oh, my Lord!" my mother exclaimed, clasping her hands over her heart. "By chance, your real name wouldn't be Saint Nickolaus?" she joked.

"Far from it," he replied. A pleased smile over our awed reaction lit up his face.

Papa insisted that Morris sit in his leather chair, and put another shovel full of coal on the fire to heat water for coffee. Mama brought out some rolls she had baked two days before. "Sorry, we don't even have cookies or a piece of cake to offer you," she apologized.

"No, no. I don't want anything," Morris replied. "You keep what you have. I don't need it." He laughed, patting his round belly.

Papa's English had remained limited to just a few words, and he even got those mixed up, saying hello when he meant goodbye, and vise versa, but Mama and I translated for him. We asked Morris where he lived in the States and listened fascinated as he told us of Los Angeles, Hollywood, the Pacific Ocean, and a year-round summer sun. He did not like the cold, raw weather here in Germany, and looked forward to returning home. "Two more months," he said with a sigh.

"How long have you been over here?" my father wanted to know.

"Since D-day."

"Then you have seen a lot," my mother said, nodding her head, looking at him thoughtfully.

"That I have."

For an awkward long moment our conversation paused as each of us seemed to reflect on that last and bloodiest year of the war. Mama broke the silence by offering Morris a refill of coffee.

"No, no. Thanks Mom." Morris said and held up his hands. "I must get back to the base." He rose out of the chair, tucked up his belt, then put an arm around Mama's shoulders.

"I'll come again. OK?"

"OK." Mama smiled up at him. She looked so small and frail beside him, fitting easily under his arm.

Morris said goodbye, shaking Papa's extended hand, and I walked with him out to his jeep.

"Maybe you can arrange for me to meet this dealer we had talked about?" he asked.

"I'll try," I promised.

Before climbing into his vehicle, he turned around, grabbed my shoulders, flashed his eyebrows and made a couple of clicking sounds. "See you later, babe," he said, then took off.

I watched his jeep roar down the street and disappear around a corner.

Two afternoons later, the doorbell rang, and there was Morris again. This time he brought with him canned bread pudding and peaches. "If somebody ever asked where you got this stuff, don't give them my name," he grinned, "or I'll go to the clink instead of home."

That day, after he had left, Papa asked me, "What did you say his name was?"

"Morris Katz," I answered.

"Katz? That sounds like a Jewish name."

Oh, I wished Papa had not said anything. Suddenly, I felt tense and uncomfortable in Morris' presence. He is Jewish, yet, he is so nice to us? Every day new headlines condemned Germans for the torture and death of millions of Jews. The German press reported mostly what foreign papers had written about us. Emotionally, this stung and bruised more than a lashing could. It also definitely influenced many Americans in the way they treated us. I wished to find the courage to ask Morris what he thought and how he felt.

To show our deep appreciation for Morris' generosity, Mama invited him to share our New Year's dinner. He accepted and showed up with a box of cigars for Papa, and a big bar of chocolate each for Mama and me. The dinner was not quite ready and the kitchen was still a mess.

"Go, entertain Morris in your room while Papa and I finish here," Mama said. "Papa built a fire in your stove, it should be warm in there by now." In the summer, my room often doubled as a living room when we had company. In the winter, we seldom used it because of a lack of fuel to heat it.

Morris looked around my room and saw the pictures of Willi and Pepi. "Brother? Sweetheart?" he asked.

I nodded and told him a little about each one. "Both of them are dead. Killed in action," I explained.

Morris said nothing. After awkward moments of silence, he turned to a chessboard on my dresser, changing the subject. "Who plays? Do you?"

"My father and I play sometimes. He is a master at it," I said. "Do you want to play?"

"Sure," he said, "but you'll probably beat the socks off me."

"I'm not that good. Haven't been able to beat my father yet," I assured him.

I moved the board to the table, took two pawns, one white, one black, hid one in each fist and held them out for Morris to choose. "Right or left?" I asked. He drew the black one. It was my start.

The first few moves did not take much concentration. We talked a little about how each of us survived New Year's Eve. He said that he went to bed shortly after midnight, but noisy revelers kept him awake as they reeled into the barracks.

116

"I did a show," I told him. "Afterwards we stayed for a big party and danced until midnight. GIs were allowed to bring their German girlfriends. At twelve o'clock the music stopped and everybody shouted 'Happy New Year' and popped balloons. It was crazy, but fun. I got home really late. "Actually," I laughed, "it was early morning when I got home."

While I prattled on about the party, inwardly I felt tight as a drum. There were questions I wanted to ask Morris but did not know how. I wanted to know what he, as a Jewish person, thought about Germans. Sometimes I caught him gazing at me and wondered if, perhaps, he wrestled with the same topic. Why did he go out of his way to be so nice to us?

"Check," he said, startling me back to the game.

"Oh, my...I didn't see that." My mental wanderings had cost me a knight.

"You are not concentrating. Got something on your mind?"

"Guess I just partied too hard last night," I laughed, avoiding his eyes.

I was glad when Mama called us to the table.

Before Morris sat down, he looked at the food with interest, asking what it was and how it was made. Mama explained as she dished each item onto his plate. "These are potato dumplings made from cooked potatoes; this is sweet-sour red cabbage; and this is called *Gaenseklein*, a favorite, traditional New Year's dish in Bavaria."

"It all looks and smells delicious." He wanted to know more about the *Gaenseklein*. "What's it made from?"

"Parts from the goose such as the neck, giblets and wings, marinated in a brine of vinegar and spices," Mama explained. She did not mention the feet and the head.

"Well, I'll try anything once," Morris replied, not too sure at first. We watched his reaction as he took the first few bites. "Hey...that's not bad," he said and nodded approvingly. Mama and Papa beamed, each crediting their individual touches for the good taste. Morris liked it so much that he asked for a second helping. Nothing could have pleased Mama more. "Of course, of course," she encouraged him, putting another dumpling on his plate, and shoving the bowl with the *Gaenseklein* closer to him so he could help himself. Morris dipped the ladle in and came up with the goose's head. He froze and stared at it, then looked at us and let the ladle sink back into the dark brown gravy. "On second thought, I really have had enough," he said and gulped, "but I would like a glass of water." The expression on Morris' face said it all.

"*Das ist gut...das ist gut,*" Papa tried to convince him.

"It's a delicacy," Mama added, perturbed over his reaction. "It used to be served in the best restaurants."

"Sorry, Mom," he said and shoved the plate away from him.

"So am I, Morris, I should have warned you," I said. "I remember what it's like, when I stared at my first plate full of snails in France. I couldn't understand how anybody could eat such slimy, crawly things as snails. With a lot of coaxing I finally tried some and eventually I actually learned to like them. Do you like snails?"

"Snails I can eat, but not something that's staring back at me," Morris replied with half of a grin, squirming in his seat.

"I've heard that you eat rattlesnakes in America."

"Not me. Cowboys might."

Morris recovered from the shock and the conversation turned lighthearted as we compared and laughed at the various differences in cultures, not just about food, but also about customs and habits. "I've had to get used to this business of shaking hands with every German I meet," Morris chuckled, "and having to tip an attendant before using a toilet in a public place."

When Morris left that day, I was relieved that he seemed to have taken no offense to the dinner surprise. Before he took off in his jeep, I gave him a peck on the cheek. "What's that for?" he asked.

"Just to say thanks. Not just for the things you brought. Thanks for being you."

Our eyes met, lingered, as if to look into one another's soul. His head nodded slightly as he said, "You are all right, kid. You are all right. So are your folks." Then he drove off.

I did not know why, but his words moved me so that I ran into the house, into my room and cried. It was as if someone had lifted a mountain off my shoulders.

Morris kept visiting my family and me until the day he shipped out. At our final goodbye, I told him teary-eyed how much his friendship meant to me in light of all this guilt being heaped on us.

"Don't let it bother you. You folks are all right. Don't worry. Eventually, the good guys get sorted out from the bad."

"I hope so, Morris. I hope so."

Many times thereafter I had to think back on his parting words, still waiting for the 'sorting out.'

Chapter 9

Reunions

$\mathfrak{D}$eep snow covered the wounds of the city like cotton dressing. Above the muted sound of traffic floated the bell-like laughter of children pulling and riding their sleds up and down a small hill, a sound not heard for several years. Most of these children had been evacuated to small villages in upper Bavaria to escape the bombing. I stopped and watched them play. The winter air had painted their cheeks and noses pink. Snow crusted their hats, mittens and coats, melting from the warmth of their bodies, soaking through to their skin, no doubt. In the heat of play, they seemed oblivious to it.

How well I remembered once playing on these same hills, coming home afterwards, soaked and freezing, changing clothes in front of a glowing kitchen stove, where Mama heated a cup of milk or cocoa for me. I wondered to what these children returned? There would be no fire in the kitchen stove, if they were lucky enough to still have one. At best, there would be the arms of a loving mother wrapping a blanket around her shivering, hungry child.

The war was over, yet, the suffering continued. Looking at the total devastation around me, I could not imagine that life in Munich could ever be pleasant again. Not in my lifetime, I thought. It took eight hundred years for this city to rise and evolve to what it was, a gateway across the Alps, to east and west. Its easy pace and unvarnished charm drew people from all over the world to relax and have fun, while enjoying a vast array of art and intellectual offerings. The city was unrecognizable now. People who had lived here all their lives got lost, not knowing what street they were on.

Before the war, Munich had been called the 'City with a Heart.' Its pulse could be felt regularly at a place called *Platzl*, a small theater right across from the famous *Hofbrauhaus*, with its lowbrow *Gemuetlichkeit* where native sons like Valentin and Weissferdl poked fun at the world. Even Nazi big shots had been seen in the crowd, laughing, though they were often the subjects of the jokes. A couple of times these humorists had been arrested for gross insubordination, but their immense popularity affected their release and kept them out of concentration camps. Of course, their humor had died with the city.

January and February used to be months of *Fasching* (Mardi Gras), when jesters ruled and costumed merrymakers roamed the streets. From prestigious organizations, to churches, to neighborhood pubs, everybody staged a *Faschingsball* (masquerade ball). Even priests got caught up in this pagan madness, donned outlandish duds and joined the fun. And madness it was. My sixty-five year old aunt had worked hard all day, then gone to a ball and partied all night, and did this sometimes for three consecutive days. I was only a child

121

and wondered why she did not keel over from lack of sleep.

This also used to be a busy time for me as a child, performing at many such balls. I loved it. The colors, the fantasy, the flirting, people acting out what their costumes represented...it was such a fun time, a time of make-believe. This frenzied carnival culminated in the last three days before Ash Wednesday with a grand parade through downtown Munich, dancing in the streets, and total craziness around the clock. Mouth watering aromas of freshly fried *Faschingskrapfen*, a kind of donut-like dumpling, drifted from bakeries and households onto the streets. Street vendors offered an unlimited supply of confetti, serpentines, ratchets and noisemakers. Immersed in this exhilarating pandemonium of music, laughter, and noisemaking, entangled in brightly colored streamers, wading ankle-deep in confetti, I could not wait until I was grown up to fully participate in this revelry. But then the war started. This madness stopped, as did the laughter, replaced by madness of another kind that produced only tears.

"Don't think about what was," I scolded myself. "It's gone. Nothing can roll back time." I locked away these memories like outgrown toys in an attic trunk, and concentrated on the present and on how to survive.

As I kept on working for the Americans, I ran into two of my former colleagues from the Molkow Ballet. We had spent a couple of years together on tour through Germany and its neighboring eastern zones, the Russian front, and France. A year before the war's end, I was forced to leave the company because of illness, and in the chaos of Germany's collapse I had lost touch with the troupe. First I met Uschi. She was the guest of an American colonel at an officer's club where

I performed. We talked briefly after the show, and then again the next morning before the show was being trucked back to Munich. Uschi was originally from Koenigsberg, East Prussia, which was now in Russian hands.

After I had left the dance company, it had continued traveling through Belgium, Hungary and Greece. Uschi described the harrowing last months, trying to get back to Germany and arriving in Berlin only weeks before the Russians did. Shot at, wounded, sick with diarrhea, she and the others in the company had trekked all the way from Crete, Greece over the Alps to Berlin on foot, on donkey carts, in fishing boats, by truck and train with nothing more than the clothes on their backs.

"I could have stayed in Berlin with Molkow, like some of the others did," Uschi said, "but I wanted to find my family before the end came." Molkow, the director of the company, lived in a big villa in a suburb of Berlin.

"And did you find them?" I asked.

"No." Uschi looked down to the floor, shaking her head. Her chin quivered and she fought back tears. "I still don't know where they are, what happened to them. They got trapped in the Russian zone."

"How did you wind up here in Bavaria?"

"With the colonel." Uschi's head tilted toward a closed door at the small, second floor apartment where she stayed. She continued, "I trekked south with other refugees when advancing Americans stopped us and asked for someone who could interpret for them. I volunteered and have been with the colonel ever since."

"You live with him?" I tried to sort this out. Uschi was twenty-four, the colonel in his fifties. She shrugged her shoulders.

"Why not? At least I have a roof over my head, enough to eat, and he even got me the clothes I wear. What else can I do? Where can I go? It's better than staying in Berlin, getting raped by Russians."

Having a flashback, I saw five-foot Uschi kissing the six-foot something Prince of Prussia, standing on tiptoes on the running board of his vehicle, stretching up to him as he stooped to meet her lips. That happened when we entertained German troops at the Russian front, when neither of us expected to come out alive.

"Did you ever hear from the prince again?" I asked.

"He visited us between tours in Berlin, at Molkow's house," she answered with a reminiscent smile.

I was pleased to hear that he had survived. When he and other royals had been recalled to Berlin, we had feared the worst for them.

As Uschi and I parted, we promised to stay in touch, but I never saw or heard from her again.

Not long after that, at another show, I met Ulla, also one of the dancers with the Molkow Ballet. She was the sister of our director's wife and for quite a while the soloist of the company until I took her place. She never forgave me for that, and our relationship was cool at best. When I met her again, she was the assistant to a famous, incredible contortionist. From her, I learned that all who had stayed at the Molkows' villa had survived. For weeks, the women hid in the basement of the house where raiding Russians eventually found them and raped Ulla's eighty-year old grandmother and her sister.

"They dragged me up the stairs by my feet and..." Ulla stopped in mid-sentence. Her expression suddenly changed as if someone had thrown a switch and turned out the lights. "I must go," she said abruptly. "I'm sure we'll bump into each other again."

I had still so many questions, but she left.

124

In the meantime, my folks got word that the Hilsenbecks had returned, for whom my father had worked until they fled from the Gestapo. At one time they were neighbors and spent many evenings at our house. Herr Hilsenbeck was a maverick, his wife a soft-spoken mystic. I loved them both because they always seemed to generate excitement. Sometimes, I was allowed to stay up when they came over. Herr Hilsenbeck frequently coaxed my parents and some friends into holding seances. They sat around the kitchen table with their hands atop a footstool that tapped out messages from the beyond. He called up his wife's deceased sister and the dead from hell, whereupon the footstool began to knock violently. I had seen it jump and fly through the air. One time, this so scared my 300-pound aunt that she jerked backwards on her stool and crashed to the floor. At the beginning of these sessions, our cat, napping at his usual spot atop the kitchen buffet, suddenly rose and looked around the room with wide, frightened eyes. He saw something we could not. His fur bristled. He humped his back, hissed, then took flight, hiding in the farthest corner under the stove.

Herr Hilsenbeck did not do this for entertainment; he was curious and wanted to connect with another dimension he seriously believed existed. He seemed to have succeeded beyond his expectations. One morning, my mother and I stopped at his place to pick up Frau Hilsenbeck to go shopping with us, and found their apartment turned upside-down by unknown forces, furniture and all.

"Are you moving?" was the first thing my mother asked.

"No," Frau Hilsenbeck replied, with a bewildered look on her face. "This all happened in the middle of night. I woke up hearing something fall to the floor, chairs being moved, and drawers being opened. I woke my husband, thinking it was an intruder. He got up and armed himself with a brass candlestick. Suddenly, burners on the gas stove lit up, yet we saw no one strike a match to light them. Someone threw a coat at him, still on a hanger." She paused, brushed back strands of her uncombed hair, then resumed sweeping up broken glass and dishes. "Once we were up, everything was quiet again. The door was still locked. I have a hunch it was my sister's spirit."

I can still see that room. A huge, three door, mirrored armoire had been moved from its place along a wall and stood cockeyed in the center of the room. The drawers and contents of a large dresser cluttered the floor. Pictures on the walls hung askew as if after an earthquake.

"Look at this," Frau Hilsenbeck pointed to a large Chinese vase sitting on the table. "It was a gift from my sister. I had it sitting on the floor next to the armoire, and this morning I found it undamaged, sitting on the table. What do you make of that?"

My mother's jaw hung open. She could only shake her head.

I was more intrigued than frightened by this, and it persuaded me more than any religious teachings did to believe in mystic forces and the possibility of a hereafter. While I cannot explain the causes of what I saw and experienced, I cannot deny it. It happened. It was real, and kept me from becoming a total skeptic.

After fleeing from the Gestapo, the Hilsenbecks sat out the last years of war in Switzerland. They had done well. Herr Hilsenbeck was involved in metallurgical research for a large company. He was also an active World Citizen and had learned to speak 'Esperanto,' a new, artificial language that was to unite the world. One of the first things he did when we met again, was

126

to lecture us on this subject: "It's the only way to prevent another war." He preached with conviction. "We must all become citizens of one world, instead of one or the other country."

I had always idolized him as some kind of genius, and listened to what he had to say. But I was no longer a child, and, drawing from my own experience, I could no longer agree with everything he said. I pictured the world he proposed, a world without borders, with the same language, thrown together like a pot of stew, and felt sad. "Do we need to make everything the same just to avoid war? Could we not learn to appreciate each other's differences? The Italians would not be Italians, the Russians not Russians, the French not French anymore. All art would look alike, music sound alike." What he proposed sounded like a nightmare to me. "And who would govern this world?" Herr Hilsenbeck had answers for everything, but I remained skeptical.

He had returned to Germany not just to visit his old homeland; he came to do business and set up metal collection centers all over the city to help with the rebuilding of it. Sorted, the metals could be melted down and reused. He asked my parents to run such a place, and since the insurance business my father was in had collapsed, he accepted. It later turned into a thriving business for a while.

Winter turned into spring. I had become good friends with Chicosh, the Hungarian violinist at the Dachau officers' club. He was still held prisoner there. At night he played for the Americans at various clubs; during the day he was part of a work detail to do whatever the Amis needed to have done. One day he mentioned that an officer wanted to get rid of an old piano in his quarters. He just wanted it out. All my life I had wanted a piano. I took lessons as a child from a crabby, eighty-year old lady, a former opera singer, who lived in an apartment above ours, then had to practice on a paper keyboard my father had drawn for me. I hated it, but I learned to read music, and needed it later to pass my state exam as a dancer.

For a few packs of cigarettes, I had the piano delivered to my house. Made from cherry wood, the piano was beautiful, but needed repair and tuning. The musician who had transposed and orchestrated the music for all my present dance numbers, was glad to oblige. He still lived with his wife and four children in one room and was desperate to provide for them. I also took lessons from him.

The piano marked a milestone in my life. Growing up, I had been exposed to many different lifestyles, mostly better and more cultured than ours. It began when I modeled for professors at the arts academy in Munich at the age of four. Professor Best and Professor Funk lived in villas brimming with art, from Persian rugs over inlaid floors, statues in the foyer, carved railings, carved furniture, gold rimmed dishes and delicate Chinese tea sets, to a studio and library filled with tangible and intangible treasures. Later, in grade school, a volunteer program selected and matched children from poor families with families of the upper middle class, to have dinner with them once a week, not only to get a good meal, but to learn etiquette. This exposure made me so very aware of my family's poverty that I was often embarrassed to bring my friends home, but it also constantly reinforced a strong desire to rise above it someday. Now I had a piano. It was not a grand, but it was a piano, and when I ran my fingers over it, it actually responded with sound, not like the keys my father drew on a strip of paper. I was rich...I was rich. The piano meant as much to me as the leather chair did to my father.

My joy, however, was riddled with guilt. I had a piano now; so many other people still did not have a roof or bed.

When our neighbors saw the piano being delivered and carried in off an Ami truck, tongues wagged anew. Then, minutes into my first lesson, the tenant above us, that nitpicking old bureaucrat, started pounding on his floor so hard that I thought the ceiling would come down. I tried to negotiate with him for a time when my lessons and practice would not bother him. Impossible. I played my lessons pianissimo, and practiced when I saw him leave the house.

My friend, Chicosh, looked forward to his release, to return to Budapest where he planned to reenter the university to study medicine. He seemed to be very much liked and trusted by the Americans, and usually assigned to the better jobs. Shortly before his release, he was called to help General Eisenhower, who was leaving Europe, pack his belongings to be shipped to the United States. It was a bigger job than he thought. "You should have seen the great paintings and art treasures we had to crate up. A truckload full," he told me, shook his head and shrugged his shoulders. "To the victor belong the spoils."

"It's only wrong when Germans do that. Might makes right," I quoted my father.

Meantime, we also received the first mail from my mother's sisters in the USA. GIs like Bob and Harry had kept their promise and dropped off the letters we sent with them. We had not been in touch with Mama's sisters since the war started and were overjoyed to hear from them. In turn, they were happy to learn that we had survived. Later, we received a couple of CARE packages from them.

Working for the Americans became less and less appealing. We had to travel ever-greater distances, always on trucks, and the Special Service no longer provided housing for us. They left that to our agents. The places available to us, to Germans, often ranked lower than stables where clean straw would have been more inviting. We also no longer received cigarettes. When the Amis caught on what cigarettes could buy—diamonds, jewelry, Swiss watches, rare antiques—they hoarded them for themselves. The black market flourished more than ever. Black marketeers drove around in gleaming automobiles, dressed in hand tailored shirts and suits, with diamond studded cufflinks and tiepins. Among them were many foreign workers from former labor camps. No one bothered these outlaw-merchants unless one of them swindled a high-ranking Ami. Only the starving public, people coming back on trains from the country with a few eggs, a little bacon, butter or a chicken, were arrested, fined, and had their precious bartered goods taken from them, and not by the Amis, but by the German police. "Shame on you," people would heckle them. "Why don't you go after the big guys?" Because the German police did this to other Germans especially riled the public. "Give a German orders, you can be sure that they will be carried out," they mocked in cynical self-recognition.

We were lucky to still have American friends. Billy the Greek, young and handsome, orphaned as a child, had found in us a family he always longed for. Captain Smith, who was so homesick for his wife and young child, who said I reminded him of her, remained a friend for many years. Many others came and went, transferred after only a short acquaintance. I have thought of them many times since with a grateful heart. They helped us through the roughest times.

Chapter 10

Oh, What a Tangled Web We Weave!

From time to time, my spirit slumped into dark depression. We had no name for it then. I moped around the house, did not want to talk to anybody, and often wished I would not wake up to face another day. "What's the matter with you?" my mother nagged. "Your chin is dragging on the floor." I did not know myself what ailed me. To avoid her probing, I took off for the woods, weather permitting, and sat for hours under some tree, letting my thoughts ride the wind. The stillness seemed to soothe an aching emptiness within me.

I was twenty now, and without a vision. My career as a dancer, for which I sacrificed so much and trained so hard, had lost its glamour. And the death of Pepi, the soldier I had met in Russia, with whom I was deeply in love, had broken my heart. For two years, in almost daily letters, letters ten or more pages long, we had planned and dreamed of a future together. Once the war was over we would get married and live in Vienna.

He would return to the academy of music; I would keep on dancing. Eventually we would have a family, raising our children in a house filled with music and love. With him gone, so was my blueprint for the future. I lived life without a map, without a tomorrow, without meaning.

Subconsciously, I searched for Pepi in every man I met. Initially attracted by a gesture, a certain look or laugh, I found quickly that all similarities usually ended there. Because I worked for Americans, most men I met were Americans. German fellows, the few that had survived the war, held me in contempt for keeping company with them. In their eyes, I was being disloyal to our veterans, who had fought, bled and died for us. I understood their hurt. They had done their duty as good men do when called upon to fight for their country, not unlike their American counterparts. The only difference between them was that one side won and the other lost.

On stage and in public, no one could have guessed that my 'self' was dying. I was, after all, a performer. "Laugh, even if your heart is breaking." My friends and colleagues knew me as a strong, fiercely independent spirit, to be called upon to resolve dicey situations. I could share laughs and tears with them, but not the flutterings of my soul.

Out of the public's eye, that mask fell off. Each day seemed to begin and end in futility.

Then I met the Dubskys, a large circus family from Hungary.

First, I met the grandfather of the Dubsky family. Small, thin, and still quite agile in his sixties, he was a knife thrower, sword-swallower and flame-spewer. His act, assisted by his wife, occasionally was booked with our show. I could not watch it. It made me too nervous, especially when he threw knives at the board

132

where his wife posed, where the blades landed less than an inch from her body.

The Dubskys had flooded into Bavaria with thousands of other refugees from the east, competing for the already stressed resources. All had to be housed. All had to be fed. Some native Bavarians resented bitterly what they perceived as their preferential treatment by the American run government, and did not hesitate to express their feelings openly. Sadly, already driven from their homes, robbed of all they owned, these refugees frequently became the scapegoats for all the ills of those trying times.

Scattered during the chaotic last months of the war, caught behind newly drawn borders, the Dubsky family gradually found their way back together. It had grown to nine, with several members still missing. Its latest additions were two young men who had escaped Russian captivity. All were performers, acrobats, tumblers, jugglers, aerialists, and musicians. Together, they immediately worked up a variety of very good acts. When they had enough for a full show, they broke ties with our agent and struck out on their own. As Hungarians they were privileged to stay in American quarters, eat in American canteens, get American money and buy in the PX.

One day, the Dubskys approached me with an offer to join their show. "We could use a good dancer in our show," father Dubsky said. "Join us. We'll claim you as one of our daughters and get a pass for you with Hungarian papers from one of our own, still missing daughters."

"But I don't speak the language. What, if the Amis find out?"

"We'll teach you a few phrases. As long as we have papers for you, and you don't tell anyone, we should be all right."

My heart hammered in my throat. What they offered me was heaven. But the risks...the risks! I remembered the night in jail, the pathetic scene of a powerless, wretched mass of people who had done no wrong, shaking in their shoes in front of the hostile judge. But the lure of breaking the chains of defeat with its shame and guilt, of living like a human being again, was just too great.

Another incentive was Nicki, the Dubsky's youngest son, whose fiery, dark eyes followed me around where ever I went. His youthful, exuberant presence made me feel alive again. Lean and strong, he could pick me up over his head and whirl me around as if I were a toy. We teased and romped like puppies; I learned to laugh again. He even looked a little like Pepi.

I took the risk. The first time I performed with the Dubskys was at a resort village in the Swabish Alps. As soon as we arrived there, American army personnel helped us settle into a small hotel overlooking the park-like grounds of a spa. I had a room all to myself. It was heated. The linen on the bed smelled of fresh mountain air and sunshine, and was as white as new snow. Just a few steps down a carpeted hallway was the bathroom where we could take hot baths or showers, with soap and towels provided. Taking immediate advantage of these facilities, I cleaned up, then threw myself onto my bed, luxuriating in its clean, downy softness.

Downstairs, in a small, comfortable lobby with a fireplace and bar, the German staff catered to us with coffee and drinks, as they may have done once with wealthy spa guests. Later, we dined at the officer's mess across the street, in the elegant, former dining hall of the spa. I did not let on that I was German, speaking only English or using Hungarian words and phrases within earshot of the staff.

Except for the Americans in their olive-brown uniforms, nothing in that village reminded one of the war. It was as if I had awakened from a nightmare. My chest swelled. I felt suddenly rejuvenated and inches taller. This exhilarating experience only made me hunger for more.

My earnings improved life at home also, put food on the table, coal on the fire, and allowed us to buy on the black market such dire necessities as facial soap, razor blades, laundry powder, leather soles for our tattered shoes, an inner tube for my father's bike, and a long list of other every-day essentials. I was grateful to the Dubsky's, who treated me as if I really were one of their own.

From time to time, I ran into people who knew me. "How come you get to eat and stay with the Americans? You are German, just like we are." This resulted in a few scuffles when I entered a building or facility and others could not. What saved me was that the Americans did not understand German, and most Germans spoke very little English. However, this experience left me shaken. If exposed, we all could land in jail, and not just for a day, but for years.

At one of our bookings, we crossed paths with an American road show. A man from the advance team, a corporal in the Special Service, invited us to see the play "My Sister Eileen." He had his eye on me, and did this as a gesture to impress us of his importance. I did not like this guy; yet, he followed me around like a bloodhound. Nicki teased me, "Now, there is a man for you—a whale of a man." He referred to the corporal's size that bulged in the seams of his uniform, and hung in rolls over his belt. Nicki liked to show off his physical prowess in front of him by lifting me upon his shoulder, or doing a handspring right over our heads.

135

"This is your brother?" the corporal asked suspiciously, watching the glances flying back and forth between Nicki and me.

"Well, yes," I answered.

The corporal, whose name was Robert, joined us at every meal, bringing father Dubsky cigars, and chocolates for the women, telling us of his privileged life in the States. He passed around pictures and news clippings of his father, a distinguished, important looking gentleman, and of his parents' home. Turning to me he said, "I would love to take you back home with me. With my connections to Hollywood, I could make you a star."

"Oh, yeah?" I replied mockingly. "Where have I heard that before?" Nicki either poked or kicked me under the table. I did not dare look at him or we would have burst out laughing.

Not only did this man hang around us morning, noon and night, his pursuit of me became more intense, while I tried my best to avoid him.

"Don't you have a job or duties to perform?" I asked him once.

"I don't care. I'd go AWOL to be with you," he answered.

Most disturbing was when he scoured up other Hungarians and introduced them to me. They would say something to me in Hungarian and I did not understand a word of it.

"I thought you are Hungarian," Robert questioned.

"I was raised with relatives in Germany. We did not speak Hungarian at home," I lied, but I knew he was catching on.

Our show had worked out of Heidelberg at the time, and so did the one Robert was with. I was very glad when our stay there ended and we could leave the area. I thought this would be the end of him and hoped never to see him again, especially since his advances became more ardent and repulsively physical with each passing day. The night before we returned to Munich, he cornered me in the dark between stage and dressing room, and pressed his bulk against me, panting, "You are driving me crazy. I have to have you." He let up when he heard someone coming, and I slipped away. When I told Nicki, he threatened to lay him flat.

Unfortunately, this was not the end of the fat man. Through his connection with the Special Service, Robert knew when and where we performed. I now received hand-delivered messages from him, declaring his undying love for me, with apologies for succumbing to his passion.

Weeks later, our show was booked into Stuttgart. Like most German cities, Stuttgart lay in ruins. Few and far between stood a building that bombs had missed, occupied now by Americans. One was a five-story hotel near downtown, restored by Americans to peacetime standards, where we stayed. Again, I had a room to myself with steam heat and hot and cold running water. These days, I was giddy with happiness. My self-confidence swelled to the point of making me act cocky. When I looked in the mirror now, I saw a svelte young woman, clean and well groomed, with shiny, dark hair flowing in waves around her shoulders, wearing a stunning, new black and white checkered wool suit Frau Klara had tailored for me out of cloth purchased on the black market. It was the first new addition to my wardrobe in eight years. Frau Klara also took a white, silk parachute an Ami friend gave me, added bits and pieces of lace and sewed it into the prettiest lingerie I could imagine. What she could not do was eliminate the numbers stamped all over the silk, so, she made them part of the design. I was ecstatic. At home, I put it on and stepped in front of the mirror, dreaming, wishing I could have worn it for Pepi's return. All of this was possible only because I had papers that said I was Hungarian.

The Dubskys and I had dinner in the dining room of the hotel. Nicki sat beside me, dumping pepper into my soup until my eyes watered. "Hungarians like it hot," he teased. He was so much fun. It seemed as if both of us tried to make up for the childhood and adolescence we had missed out on because of the war. As a circus family, the Dubskys never really had a home base. Caught in Poland when the war started, they scattered. Young men were forced into the German army or, with all the rest, had to work in German factories.

We were sitting around an elegantly set table—at that time, elegant meant anything that was clean, undamaged and coordinated like the matching, unchipped porcelain on the freshly laundered table linen, with shining flatware and glasses. As we sat there, waiting to be served dessert, who would stroll into the dining room, beaming from ear to ear? "Robert!" We gasped his name like calling an alarm.

"When you weren't in your rooms, I figured I could find you here," he greeted us, pulled up a chair and sat down next to me. "Our show is staying here, too."

My stomach knotted.

"You look great, sweetheart," he said to me and put his hand on my thigh with a familiarity that raised father Dubsky's eyebrows.

"Thank you," I snapped, and brushed his hand away. Nicki raised his forearm with his hand tightening into a white-knuckled fist. Ignoring it, Robert said that he might get shipped out and only had a week left in Germany.

"Well, that's wonderful that you get to go home," I said with honest enthusiasm, thinking that I would then be rid of him for good.

"I want to marry you, before I go," Robert said and squeezed my hand. "Please, say that you'll marry me."

"Sure. Sure," I answered and burst out laughing, taking it as a joke. No American soldier could just get married, not even to an American woman without due process and approval from the army, and not at all to a German woman.

"I'll make the arrangements then," Robert beamed.

"You do that. And don't forget the ring," I mocked.

"And I'm gonna be best man," Nicki added.

Everyone around the table added bits of silliness to keep the laughter going. Robert laughed right along with us, then excused himself.

We did not see him again that day, or the next. Good, I thought, maybe he is gone. On the third day, I had gone to my room after lunch and was sitting on my bed, leafing through an American magazine I had found in the lobby, when a bellboy knocked and informed me that I was wanted at the desk downstairs. In the elevator, going down, I ran into other Dubskys, who had also been called to the desk. We wondered what was up. In the back of my mind always lurked the fear of being found out about falsifying my identity.

The elevator door opened onto the lobby. At first glance I saw a small gathering of people, in uniform and civilian clothes, and in their midst stood Robert.

"Oh, no! There he is again," I gasped.

Robert saw us. "Here you are," he greeted us and approached hurriedly. His face beamed. "I've got everything ready," he said to me. "I got a chaplain, and I got the ring."

"No...no!" My legs seemed to fill with lead, my body turned to stone. This no longer was a joke.

Robert took my arm and tried to lead me toward the group who stared at us expectantly. I did not budge. I looked at the Dubskys, at Nicki, who all seemed as stunned as I was.

"Come, come! They are all waiting," Robert urged.

"You are out of your mind!" It was all I managed to say to him as I struggled out of his hold.

A minister in clerical garb joined us. "Well? Everything is ready. If you are, we can begin," he said in broken English.

"I have no intentions of marrying this man," I told him. My voice sounded hoarse and shaky.

"Robert here said that you gave him your yes. Did you not?"

"It was a joke...it was just a joke."

"Marriage is a holy sacrament, not a joke," the minister reprimanded me. "Nor is it right to toy with someone's sincere affection. After all, this man offered you his hand in marriage."

His words stirred up a gamut of emotions, anger, embarrassment, fear, even guilt, but it was fear that overwhelmed all others. What, if he knows that I am German? What if I refuse and he takes revenge, having me and the Dubskys arrested for falsifying my papers? Breaking into tears, I asked the minister to speak with him in private. "Can I depend on your confidence?" I asked him. He nodded, reluctantly. I explained the situation to him, from joining the Dubskys to Robert's unwanted attention. While the minister's face remained expressionless, his eyes darted nervously back and forth between Robert, the Dubskys, the group of people and me. It seemed as if time stood still. Everybody held their breath and stared at us.

Humiliated, embarrassed, racked with fear of possible consequences, and with guilt for getting myself and, perhaps, the Dubskys, into this mess, I apologized to the minister and asked him to please help me end this fiasco.

Robert, meanwhile, paced the floor, cursing, acting angry. The minister only glanced at him in passing as he strode toward the group of curious onlookers. "Sorry," he said. "There is not going to be a wedding." He grabbed his coat and prayer book and exited the hotel, with Robert steaming after him.

"Let's go," father Dubsky urged his family and me and headed for the elevator. Upstairs, we followed him to his room to discuss this incident. "This man," father Dubsky said to me, "this man is obsessed with you. He is dangerous. God knows what he might do next. This could mean serious trouble for all of us."

"What do you think I should do?" I asked, still trembling inside.

"I know what I would like to do," Nicki said through clenched teeth and raised both fists.

"Yeah!" his brother seconded him. "Beat him up and dump him in the river."

"Quiet!" father Dubsky ordered his sons. Turning to me he said, "It would be best if you laid low for awhile. Go home. Stay out of sight. If what he says is true, that he is being shipped out in the next couple of weeks, you can come back. There is no telling what he might do. If he finds out that you are German...you go to jail, and so will we."

"I think, he already suspects," I said. "He gave me a funny look when I explained why I could not speak Hungarian."

We agreed that Nicki and his brother would take me to the station the following morning to take a train back to Munich. That evening, however, we did the show as usual and breathed a sigh of relief when Robert did not show his face.

I packed my bags before I went to bed that night, then laid there, unable to sleep, reviewing, reliving the crazy events of that day, wondering what I could, or should have done to avoid this. My conscience went into agonizing convulsions like in my childhood days, when I did something wrong and feared that my parents or teachers would find out. Then, even more than the punishment, I dreaded the embarrassment and shame. Now, I felt the added guilt for involving the Dubskys in this mess.

As I lay in bed, lights out, staring into the darkness, pondering the 'ifs' and 'buts,' I heard a knock on the door.

"Are you asleep?" It was Robert's voice. A wave of general malaise came over me as if my blood was draining out of my body. I did not answer.

"Wake up. I want to give you something," he said, knocking louder.

I knew I had bolted the door, but I slid out of bed, not making a sound, just to make sure. Yes, the door was bolted. I was relieved. Just as quietly, I returned to bed.

The knocking continued. Robert's voice became more irritated, and his request to open up more belligerent, angry and threatening.

"Do I have to call the MPs and tell them you are German?"

I cringed. Finally, silence. Had he given up? What would be his next move? My muscles remained so tensed that they started to pain.

For a long time, nothing more happened. Exhausted from tension, I sank back into my pillows and closed my eyes. Already drifting into sleep, I heard a noise like a key turning in the lock. I sat up with a jolt. The door opened, the light flicked on, and there stood Robert. Speechless, trembling like a leaf, I shrunk away from him into the corner between the wall and headboard, with the down cover drawn up to my chin.

"Don't get upset," he said calmly, and sat down on my bed. "I did not get a chance to give you this earlier." He reached into his shirt pocket and pulled out a ring. "Here, let me put this on your finger."

"How did you get in?" I was dumbfounded how he could unlock a bolted door. Where did he get a key?

Robert grinned, holding up a key and dangled it in front of my face. "Well, I still had that carton of cigarettes I was going to give the minister for performing the ceremony, but since he didn't, I gave it to the night clerk for this master key."

All the clerks and the personnel in the hotel were German. I was sold out by one of my own!

"Get out! Get out!" I squeaked. My voice had left me.

"Come on. Give me your hand. All I want to do is put this ring on your finger."

"Please, please, get out. Leave me alone. I don't want your ring. I don't care for you. I don't love you," I pleaded.

"That's all right. I love you for the both of us. Some day you will love me, too. Now give me your hand."

I sat with my knees drawn up, keeping myself covered. A tug of war ensued as he tried to pull the cover off me and grab my arm. I kicked, punched, bit and tried to scream. The weight of his body took my breath away.

Even after so many years later, I cannot bring myself to stir up the ugly details of that night, that had led me to the dumbest, worst decisions of my life, with most tragic, far-reaching consequences. I became hostage to his threats, hostage to my fears, hostage to the time and circumstance. That night I lost my dignity, my pride, my self-esteem. Most of all, I lost my will to fight. What I had left were shame and guilt. I felt unclean and disfigured.

I could not look into Nicki's eyes the next morning as he took me to the station. He sensed that something was wrong and tried to assure me that it would not be long before I could rejoin the Dubsky family.

At the time, rape was commonly considered to be a woman's fault. I could not talk about it, not to my parents, not to my friends. Their answer would be, "What do you expect? You got yourself into this situation." Then, an even darker fear surfaced. What, if I had become pregnant? Not married, having a child by an Ami soldier, I would be the scum of the earth. I would bring shame to my parents, shame that would also transfer to my child, a child that would never know its father, only that he was some American GI. A bastard child.

My father's history threatened to repeat itself. Suddenly I saw myself in his mother's shoes experiencing her agony. "But I would never abandon my child," I vowed. "Never!"

When I arrived home, I told no one what had happened and lied, saying that I was between contracts and that I really needed a little break. I anxiously awaited my period. It was days overdue. Tortured by the fear that I might be pregnant, I was relieved, nay, almost glad to see Robert show up at my door. He had traced me like a detective. Instead of shipping out, he had signed up for another two years of duty in Germany, to stay near me, he said. While I despised him for what he did, I forced myself to tolerate his presence until I knew for certain if I was or was not with child. If I was, I would have to marry him to give my child a father.

Days stretched into weeks. Still no period. That meant that I was pregnant, which, of course, was still only a calculated guess. I started being nicer to Robert, just in case. Finally, I had to tell him what I feared. He was delighted. "Don't fret, I'll stand by you," he said.

My parents did not like Robert from the beginning. His bulk was an embarrassment at a time when so many people had hungered down to skin and bones. I did not like to be seen on the street with him because people pointed their fingers and made remarks like, "Look at this guy, fat as a pig ready for slaughter." He also had a very annoying habit of retching and spitting that my mother found especially offensive. At the moment, however, he was my only support. He was the straw to save me from drowning. Maybe, I told myself, I could learn to respect him, eventually even learn to like him. After all, he came from a good family. Most likely, I reasoned, GIs behaved differently back home than they did here in occupied Germany.

When I finally found out that I was not pregnant after all, it was too late. I was too embroiled in the relationship and did not know how to break out, and it really did not seem to matter anymore.

I worked again for Baretti, my former agent, who was glad to have me back. My fear to run into the Dubskys again, who would certainly ask me some uncomfortable questions, was unfounded. They had mysteriously dropped out of sight and I was spared the embarrassment to explain my situation, especially to Nicki. Someone mentioned that they had moved on into the British zone.

Robert hung around, insisting that I introduce him as my fiancé. The first reaction usually was a stare and a "You must be kidding!" mostly because of his size. But since he seemed so totally devoted to me, most people reluctantly nodded their approval. Not so my parents. They saw through him. They saw a darkness in his character even I could not foresee.

Chapter 11

Surrender

All summer long, my parents and Herr Hilsenbeck had been looking for a place to set up a metals collection center. Finally they found one about two miles from our house, in a shed behind a bombed-out house. The owner of the property ran a horse-and-wagon delivery service and for the winter months, my parents had to share their office space with his horse. Herr Hilsenbeck furnished a scale for weighing the metals, and put up a big sign facing the street.

Business was slow in the beginning, requiring my parents to be there only a few hours twice per week. My father did the weighing and sorting, my mother kept the books. She usually walked the two miles to and fro, unless the weather was too ugly; then she reluctantly took the streetcar, complaining, "People are so rude. I am always black and blue by the time I get off from being elbowed and stomped on. And, ugh, the stench..." She grimaced and pinched her nose.

I knew what she meant. Sometimes, to the weekly meetings of the Theater Guild, when I could not ride my bike because of the weather, I had to take the street-car, also. It was always packed. At busy stops, people already mobbed the doors before the tram had come to a full stop—pushing, shoving, and trying to outmaneuver each other. The timid, the weak, or the mannered were lucky to get a foothold on the running board. I don't know what was worse, freezing and getting soaked hanging on to the outside, or being jammed in with reeking bodies, in clothes saturated with foul smelling smoke from homegrown tobacco. Tempers flared in situations like this. The stresses of the time left people short-fused.

A year-and-a-half had passed since the war's end but conditions had not improved much. Food and other commodities were as scarce as ever. Gas, coal and electricity were rationed to allow barely enough for light and for cooking. People traded their last possessions for a bag of coal, and winter had not even begun.

Meanwhile, the cleanup in Munich continued. Hand to hand, bucket by bucket, people tackled the mountains of rubble, concentrating mostly on clearing downtown streets. It seemed an insurmountable task and dangerous as well. A pick or shovel could trip one of many unexploded bombs hidden under the debris and make it go off. This still took many lives.

I regularly had to pass an old cemetery, plowed up by bombs during the last air raids. Sculls and bones, broken headstones and statues lay scattered everywhere. It looked like a movie set for a horror film and I could never pedal past it fast enough without getting goose pumps. One day, I noticed with relief that a small crew of men was at work to clean it up.

While streets were being cleared, Munich remained a gigantic rock pile. Lack of money, materials and machinery prevented any kind of structural repairs, or rebuilding. I often tried to imagine what it would be like to go downtown again and browse through well-stocked stores, to be able to buy what I wanted, or to stop in a café for coffee and cream-filled pastry. Since 1939, Germans had lived on rations that had shrunk steadily as the war raged on. I had bought my last pair of shoes in 1940. Already then the selection was limited and shelves emptied quickly. Now, even the stores were gone, buried under rubble and ashes. It would take more than a lifetime, I thought, to rebuild our cities, and the oldest and the most beautiful of buildings would be forever lost.

At meetings of the Theater Guild, I heard exciting rumors that the movie industry in *Geiselgasteig*—the Hollywood of Bavaria—would soon start up again. Many entertainers and artists had found well-paying jobs there in the past and hoped to work there again. So did I. To break into the film industry could mean security for several months at a time, with many bonuses. However, without an introduction or a connection to someone on the inside, chances to get past the front gate were slim. Old contacts had all but disappeared. Geiselgasteig had undergone denazification. Anyone previously engaged in filmmaking had been suspended during an investigation into their involvement in the Nazi party. That included a friend of mine, a playwright, who, like most everyone else, had been a party member. While he could not help me, he encouraged me to go out there and sign in. So, I did.

Geiselgasteig was nothing as I remembered it. I was eight years old the last time I played an extra in a movie with Maria Andergast and Paul Hoerbiger. Both were celebrities of the screen. Maria Andergast had played a teacher in a country school and I was one of the children in her class. The set was an alpine winter village with snow trucked in from the mountains. The chalet-type houses had only a façade, some with real, some with fake doors and windows. In the back of it was scaffolding. My well-meaning mother had dolled me up with corkscrew curls, ribbons and bows. Her effort backfired and cost me a major speaking part. It was given to a girl with braids, who looked more like a country girl.

I indulged in these memories while waiting at the front desk in a small, temporarily constructed office building. Wearing my black-and-white checkered suit with a silver fox—a gift from Robert—draped around my shoulders, I apparently made an impression on the young receptionist, who immediately announced me to whosoever occupied an adjacent office. When she reappeared, she handed me a questionnaire to fill out. Her stiff gestures, expressionless face and impersonal manner reminded me of a mannequin.

Sitting down on one of the straight-back chairs lined up along the plain office walls, I started filling in the requested information—name, address, date and place of birth, training and experience. Flipping to the next page, all question began with, "Were you ever a member of..." listing the various branches of the Nazi government. I had to laugh. These forms were hardly different from the forms I had to fill out when I applied for acceptance into the University of Munich under the Nazis. Only then, a 'no' to these questions kept me out. Now, I hoped, it would get me in. On still another page, I was asked if I had ever been arrested, been in a concentration camp or forced labor camp. I wrote down the 'Pflichtjahr' (a year of uncompensated service required of every German youth who did not attend higher schooling), and the year I had to work in a munitions factory. If that was not forced labor, what else could it be called?

I handed the filled-out forms back to the reception-ist. "Please, wait," she said in a cold and business-like manner, then disappeared again into the adjacent of-fice, shutting the door behind her.

"Funny," I chuckled to myself. "She is trying to fit a role just as I am doing." I wondered what she had to do or give up to land this job as receptionist at a movie set.

The wait was long and uncomfortable, filled with growing self-doubt. I felt pompously overdressed. I wanted to wipe the makeup off my face and stuff the silver fox into the nearest wastebasket. "This is not me. This is not me," something inside me screamed. Suddenly, the whole theater business made me sick. I was sick of wearing costumes, painting my face, smil-ing and pretending.

"Would you come in, please?" the receptionist came out to tell me.

At this moment I wanted to run, run out and keep on running, just running. Instead, I followed her through the door, where she stopped stiffly to let me enter.

Behind a massive desk, leaning and swiveling in a high-back leather chair, sat a man of substantial build with square features and graying hair, wearing an American uniform. I did not expect to be talking to an American and was taken aback. His first words, as he scanned me from top to bottom, were, "Do you speak English?" I nodded with a weak, "Yes."

With a hand gesture and a wink, he dismissed the receptionist, invited me to sit down, and picked up the questionnaire. "So, you are a dancer?" he said. "Where have you performed?"

"I am working for the Special Services," I answered.

"And before that?"

I gave him a quick run-down where and for whom I had worked, mentioning German occupied territo-ries, including Russia and France.

"And now you work for the Americans," he said with a shot of sarcasm. "You don't care who you dance for, do you?" he sneered.

"An audience is an audience," I answered, shrugging my shoulders, thinking, what did he expect? What a dumb question.

"And you never belonged to a Nazi organization? But you worked for them?"

"That is correct," I countered. I did not appreciate his sneer.

He mumbled something like, "Nobody wants to have been a Nazi." It sounded like a growl. His lips pressed together so that his chin flattened while he scribbled something on the papers in front of him. Then he rose to his feet and said, "Well, we put you on file. If we should have need for you, we contact you." With that, he showed me out the door.

Crisp winter air blasted my face the moment I stepped outside, carrying the pine scent of surrounding forests. I tightened the fox fur around my neck and walked to the tram stop less than a block away. Diffused sunlight shimmered through a hazy sky, tinting the world below a deceivingly warm yellow. A shattered, glassed-in shelter next to the rails offered little protection against the wind, and the cold from the frozen ground quickly penetrated the patched, paper-thin soles of my shoes. I looked at my watch, also a gift from Robert. It was close to noon, and at least twenty minutes before the next streetcar would arrive, if it was on schedule. Service to this suburb of Munich, consisting of elegant villas tucked in among long stretches of forests, was only every hour. Freezing, I decided to walk, at least to the next stop. The street was deserted.

The interview had left me feeling empty and dejected. Americans had taken over every facet of German life. Unlike the Russians, or the Nazis before them, they were not systematically cruel or oppressive, but they had definitely taken total control. They were the law. It was their word against ours. I felt like a stranger in my own country, or like an orphan in court-appointed custody. The Americans had taken over everything, even the movie industry. Intellectually, I understood and accepted these conditions; Germany had started the war and Germany had been defeated. However, on a personal level, it was demoralizing and not just for me. It affected the overall attitudes of the people, boosting the victors to overlord, and reducing the losers to serfdom.

At home, my parents asked how things went. I told them of the long forms I had to fill out, and the reaction of the interviewer to my 'no' answers about my party affiliations. "He did not believe me! He simply did not believe me," I repeated. "He made me feel like a weasel."

A knowing smile flashed across my father's face. He nodded quietly. My mother's face showed disappointment and dismay. "Did he say anything about the movies they are making?" she wanted to know.

"I didn't ask. I was too nervous," I told her.

She had hoped, I am sure, that a change in my employment would break Robert's influence over me. Secretly, so did I.

Often I lay in bed trying to visualize what it could or would have been like to be intimate with a man I loved, like I loved Pepi. Already one with him in heart and soul, the physical union would only have sanctified our love. In dreams I pictured how beautiful and fulfilling it would be to spend nights in his arms. To be with Robert I had to detach myself from myself. I shut down all emotions and forced my mind to wander off. All that was left to him was a body, dead inside. I was his hostage.

My parents still did not know the whole story, what had happened to me in the Stuttgart hotel, but they suspected as much. Robert seemed to worship me. "Nothing," he said, "can separate us." I was his golden trophy, jealously guarded, and if he could have, would have kept me under lock and key. He used my shame, my guilt, my fear like a gag and chain, setting me up in compromising situations, then getting me out so I would feel beholden to him again. He played the rescuer when MPs wanted to arrest me for possession of a gun, a gun he had put in my purse. Another time he stuffed money in my pocket then hid me in a closet as people were being searched for funds missing from a Polio drive. I would have been branded the thief and landed in jail. No one would have believed my innocence. I hated him for what he did, yet had to be grateful that he stood by me when I thought I was pregnant.

Another Christmas came and went, more meager than all others. Mama had saved and held back some canned goods given to us by GI friends to put a little extra on the table. Papa went to the country, but we had little to barter and he came home with only a few eggs, a little bacon and butter. We put up a small tree on my insistence, yet could not work up a holiday spirit. Constant arguments, mostly about Robert, drove my mother and me apart. She was not wrong. I just did not know what to do. She only complained, but could not offer me a plan to get out of my predicament.

On New Year's Eve 1946, I performed for the last time at the Garmisch *Rathskeller* before a star-studded audience, from General McNarney on down. The packed, large, smoke-filled hall had no stage, just a highly polished dance floor at its center, crowded in by tables and chairs. The waxed parquet felt like a sheet of ice under my feet and a few times, during my Spanish number, I almost landed in some general's lap.

During my last number, the Tango in Black and White, something must have snared my skirt. I heard it rip, and then it unraveled into a thousand silky, hair-fine threads that floated in the air like spider webs. Since I was almost at the end of my number, I finished, bowed and ran off, dragging my shredded skirt behind me. The audience laughed and applauded. For me, it marked the end.

The strongest number in my program, at least before American audiences, had been my Tango in Black and White. I could find nothing to replace my tattered costume. My waltz costume, and my silver sandals showed signs of suffering the same fate soon. Everything pointed down hill for me. It plunged me into an emotional abyss.

At home, conditions did not improve. My mother kept nagging me to get rid of Robert. He came and went like he owned the place, often using it as storage for his and his buddies' belongings and black market merchandize. This infuriated my mother. "I want him and his stuff out of my house. You tell him," she demanded. "What do you think happens if somebody finds his stuff in our home?"

Robert was conniving. He planted incriminating items in our home, just as he had done to me, so that we were afraid to raise a fuss. All he had to do was call the MP to have us arrested.

"Mama, I don't know what to do," I told her.

"You brought him; you get rid of him. He is nothing for you."

Her constant hassling stirred up old resentments. It was not just Robert that she found objectionable. She also did not like Frau Klara anymore; then started finding fault with my music teacher, expecting me to break off all contact with them. I remembered that all through childhood Mama had decided with whom I

154

could play or associate. She wanted me to select my friends only from the upper class, yet we were the poorest of the poor. If she had a falling out with neighbors or friends, she forbade me to talk to them. Even as I got older, she screened my friends, driving a wedge between me and anyone she did not like. Eventually, I rebelled, and was rebelling now in the case with Robert, which pushed me even more under his control. My father seldom interfered. When I complained to him, he only urged me to be patient and understanding because my mother was sickly and frail, and could suffer a heart attack.

Robert, in the meantime, had been transferred to a small town on the Rhein but came to visit frequently, with or without a pass or leave. He pressured me to come with him, painting a rosy picture of sunny vineyards, peaceful promenades along the river, and quaint old houses hugging the hills with little damage from the war. One day, after another big fight with my mother, at a point so low that the next step would have been to kill myself, I agreed to go with him.

Robert swapped cigarettes and instant coffee from the PX for a room for me with a vintner's family in Assmannshausen, near Ruedesheim on the Rhein. From my window, I could see the river and on the other side *Schloss Rheinstein*, a castle that had survived centuries. At a bend in the river rose Lorelei's rock from where this fabled siren lured ship captains to their death with her song—so the old story goes. Drinking in the pastoral calm and beauty of the area lifted my spirit, but at what price. The rift between my parents and me gnawed on my heart. In spite of everything, I loved and missed them. Away from home, I thought of all their loving deeds and of the sacrifices they had made for me. Months went by before I could reestablish contact with them. My mother urged me to come home, but without Robert.

One morning, I woke up feeling nauseated and sick. I blamed it on the smell of kerosene my landlady had used in place of wax to shine her wood floor. Thinking that I just needed fresh air, I dressed and went for a walk to clear my lungs in the fresh morning breeze. By noon, I started to feel better. For the next several days the same thing happened. "Oh, my God!" It hit me. "I am pregnant!"

Robert was delighted. "I hope it's a boy," he said. "There are no boys in my family to carry on the name. It would please my parents very much."

Thus far, I had learned that Robert's father was Dean of Adult Education at a Midwestern University. His mother was a teacher, his brother a colonel in the Army Air Corps, and his sister an airline stewardess. His aged grandfather was a still practicing Methodist minister. "Quite a respectable family Robert comes from," I tried to reassure myself.

Robert filed for permission to get married. "My Dad is good friends with the Governor of our State, and my brother has friends in the Pentagon. We should have no problems getting the papers through," he assured me.

At this point, I was resigned to marry Robert. I secretly vowed for the sake of our child that, if he would be decent, I would be a good wife to him. Maybe, I could even learn to love him.

I fondly remembered a good friend I had met while in Russia. He did not look like a Greek athlete either, was short and round, but was the sweetest man I had ever met. My colleagues had made fun of me because I preferred his company over several other, more handsome admirers. Surrounded by war, by unimaginable suffering and death, this man's philosophy and wisdom had guided me and lifted my spirits then, and it was serving me well ever since. "Life is like the weather," he said. "It can't rain forever; sooner or later the sun will shine again," he encouraged me. "Draw from the examples in nature. Everything moves through a cycle, and everything has a purpose. Out of the worst catastrophes often emerges something new, and wonderful, and good."

He was able to turn despair into hope. What would he be saying to me now? The war had taken him, too.

I was waiting for the rain to end. I was waiting for the sun to shine again.

Chapter 12

Between Ifs and Buts

Once I had recovered from the shock and sickness of my pregnancy, I focused on the miracle. My body cradled a new life, my very own child. With every thought, I pledged my life, my love to it. I vowed that my child would never want, never be hungry or cold, and never be alone. I would show it the wonders of nature, and kindle in it the loftier side of the human spirit. My mind formed the picture of a girl, and one day, leafing through a magazine, I saw a picture of a young woman amidst a field of wildflowers. Like a young willow yielding to the wind, everything about her was grace. I clipped it out and hung it over my bed. "That's what she will grow up to look and be like," I said to Robert.

"But that's a girl! It had better be a boy!" he answered, looking at me as if I had broken a vow.

Every night before I went to sleep, I stared at that picture, having read somewhere that such imagery can transfer to a fetus. Experience had taught me that good looks can open many doors and can smooth the trail of life.

Robert was attentive. He brought me food from the mess hall every morning and evening. During the first few months of pregnancy, I spent much of every day in bed. When I felt better toward afternoons, the spring-like weather drew me outside. I wandered up the terraced vineyards to the top of hills dotted with ancient ruins, dating back to the Roman Empire. Friendly vintners along the way proudly showed me their wine cellars carved deep into the hillside, with barrels stacked along rocky walls, some as round as I was tall. During the last year of the war and sometime thereafter, they kept entrances camouflaged to keep marauding armies out, Germans as well as Allies. I had to turn down the samples they offered me. The fumes inside these caverns were already enough to make me tipsy.

Sometimes on weekends, Robert and I took the train to Ruedesheim where he had a black market contact, a man with a slight eastern accent. He lived in a darkened, two-in-one-room apartment that looked like a scene out of the Arabian Nights, with oil lamps and candlelight reflecting off brocade-covered walls and lame curtains that separated the living area from the sleeping and working areas. A lush Persian carpet covered the floor, and leather upholstered ottomans circled a low, round table. My eyes wandered from one treasure to the next, from the carved rim of the table, to alabaster statues, gorgeous tapestry, and gold-framed paintings on the wall. Some looked like museum pieces.

My attention eventually shifted to the cigar-smoking, fast-talking black market merchant himself. Dressed in a velvet-trimmed smoking jacket, his dark hair slicked back, emphasizing his pointed profile, there was something dramatic and wickedly exciting about him and his place, something Mephisthophelean. I had the impression of having entered the devil's parlor. What on earth compelled him to create such an exotic setting, I wondered. Even stranger seemed the connection between Robert and him. I never saw them swap goods. Finally, I questioned Robert, but he was evasive and left my curiosity unsatisfied.

Our visits were short. Whatever business Robert had with this man, it was done quietly and secretly behind a curtain, and we left.

Black marketeers controlled the commerce in Germany and beyond. Though publicly denounced, there was not a soul who was not beholden to one of these dark princes. From generals, government officials, to the average man, all turned to them to satisfy both need and greed.

Weeks went by. Then months. I could not bring myself to tell my parents that I was pregnant for fear they would disown me. We were barely talking now. And I could already see and hear the people in our neighborhood whisper behind my back, pretending not to see me when I crossed their path. Though I was now twenty-one and wore Robert's ring, a pregnant, officially unmarried woman was a disgrace, even more so when the man she was involved with was a GI.

My tummy bulged early. None of my clothes fit anymore and I had to wear an apron most of the time to cover gaping skirts and blouses. Robert bought me a dress from a WAC at the enlisted men's club. Its knitted material stretched just enough to still fit over my belly. On cold days, I wore Robert's army sweater. Totally dependent on him now, I worried about how I would get diapers, clothes and blankets for the baby. He wrote home to his family. In their letters back, they

160

did not even acknowledge my existence, much less respond to his request.

Toward the end of my fourth month, I came down with a fever and for days could hold nothing in my stomach. Robert fetched a local doctor who said I had appendicitis and, unless I had immediate surgery, I could die. For a carton of cigarettes, he said, he could get me admitted at the hospital in Ruedesheim and do the surgery. I doubted his diagnosis, but he put so much fear in us that we consented. Most Germans' medical expenses were covered by state insurance, but Germany's remaining hospitals were so overcrowded that people literally died at their doorsteps waiting to get in.

Robert borrowed a jeep and drove me to Ruedesheim the following morning. On the way he told me that he had orders in his pocket to ship out within twenty-four hours. Sick, and already so weak that I could barely walk, this news wiped out what energy and will I had left within me. It even drained away my fear of the surgery. I saw myself abandoned.

Night was falling around me; I drifted into darkness. "Oh, God, just let me die," I remember praying. "It's all right. I should have died a long time ago. I am ready. Peace...peace at last...for me and my baby."

"You have to go home," I vaguely heard Robert say. "I asked the landlady to write to your parents, explaining the situation."

Home? Harsh words I had exchanged with my parents resonated like hammer blows in my heart. Away from home, I could remember only the good times, and how safe and protected I felt growing up. I missed them and loved them. Silent tears streamed down my face and neck, bitter tears, tears of regret. "If only I had...! Goodbye Mama, Pappa. I am so sorry, so sorry for the hurtful things I have said and done. I know you always meant well. Forgive me."

"I'll have a couple of buddies look in on you while you are in the hospital," Robert tried to comfort me.

Next, I remembered waking up in a hospital ward with a burning pain in my side. My first thought was about my baby. "Do I still have my baby?" I felt my belly and it was still round and firm. "Why didn't you let me die, God? How will I shelter, clothe and feed my child?"

Sunny daylight streamed in from several large windows along one wall. Everything in the room was squeaky-clean and chalk-white from ceiling to walls, to the bedding. I heard subdued voices and tried to turn to see where they came from, but a sharp pain froze me in place. A nurse in a blue-and-white striped uniform whooshed quietly back and forth past my bed. Though I was in pain, I did not want to show it. I had heard what people said about others in my situation and did not expect much sympathy. "That's what she gets for whoring around with the Amis. What can she expect? She should have known better." These thoughtless comments had angered me then. "Who are they? Saints?" I wondered what one could find out by digging into their lives. Now, I would be their target.

Pain took over my thoughts. The smell of ether oozed from every pore of my body, making me gag. Finally, a nurse stopped at my bed to look at my wound.

"Is the baby going to be all right?" I groaned.

"You don't have any contractions, do you?" she asked, concerned.

"It just hurts," I answered.

"I'll give you a shot for the pain."

"Water...can I have water?" My mouth was dry, my lips parched.

That evening the doctor stopped by. "Well, your appendix is out. It won't give you any more trouble."

"Was it really my appendix that made me sick?"

"Don't worry about it," he skirted my question. "You don't need it."

"What about my baby?"

"It'll be fine."

I could never rid myself of the suspicion that this doctor operated on me just to get his hands on a carton of cigarettes.

◆　◆　◆

A few days later, I felt the baby kicking for the first time. It affected me like a kick in the rear. I scolded myself, "Quit feeling sorry for yourself. Pull yourself together. You have responsibilities."

My hospital stay lasted five days. Robert's buddies visited me twice. They told me that Robert was stationed in Bremen now, hundreds of miles away. Upon my release, they also picked me up and drove me back to Assmannshausen. My landlady, meanwhile, had received a telegram from my father, saying he was coming to take me home.

The day of my father's arrival, I paced the floor. What would he say? Would he even talk to me? Then the moment arrived. A knock at the door. I opened it and he and I stood face to face. His stern, steely-eyed expression kept me from throwing my arms around his neck, and for a moment, we just stood there, lost for words. But in seconds, the ice in his eyes melted, and my own tears found release. We embraced and clung to one another like two castaways in heavy seas.

Had he ever thought of the similarity of his mother's fate and mine? He had held no grudge against her. Maybe he would forgive me, too.

Both of us avoided talking about Robert and my pregnancy as we prepared for the trip home. Having accumulated a few large items like a baby carriage, a wicker rocking chair, pillows and blankets, I was in a quandary as how to get them from Assmannshausen to Munich and home. My landlady told me of a man in town with a truck, who wanted to drive to Munich if he could get gas. With help from Robert's buddies, who heisted a couple of five gallon cans full of gas, the man agreed to drive us home.

The doctor had stopped by to take out my stitches. We were packed and ready to leave. Still very sore, I was not looking forward to spending five or six hours on the back of an open, dilapidated old truck. However, bedded down on pillows and blankets, with Papa sitting beside me on a footlocker, we made it home before sundown, despite rainsqualls, flat tires and an overheating engine.

Mama's reception was cool. Grief and worry were imprinted on her face. I had killed all of her dreams.

I had made up my mind not to hide my pregnancy from the public, or my friends, neighbors or colleagues. "I did what I did. I am what I am. Let those without sin throw the first stone." Little did I realize how many people fell into that category. A jovial greeting suddenly earned me, if any acknowledgement at all, a curt nod or hello. I could not concern myself with that. My focus was on preparing for the arrival of my child. My best friend, Hanni, Frau Klara, the Hilsenbecks, and singer Sefi stood by me. Frau Klara contributed cotton remnants, old sheets and shirts, to make into baby clothes and diapers. Hanni found somebody who loaned me a crib. The Hilsenbecks and Sefi helped smooth the relationship between my parents and me. Eventually my mother, unable to watch my clumsy attempts at sewing, softened and gave me a hand, too.

About every other week, I received a letter from Robert. Sometimes he enclosed a dollar or two. Considering that a hundred dollars could buy a house, even a few dollars now and then kept us afloat.

I was in my seventh month when Robert came on a three-day-pass. Just to see him again evoked the same repulsion toward him as I felt the night at the Stuttgart hotel. As we said hello, his hand immediately groped under my dress. He had only one thing on his mind, now as he did then, caring little that my parents stood right next to us. Embarrassed, I pushed him away. My God, I thought, here I am pledged to marry this man, carry his child, and am sickened by the mere sight of him. What am I going to do?

The moment he set foot into our home, trouble started anew. He brought everyone a gift—cigars for Papa, an exquisite soup terrine for Mama, and a precious porcelain figure for me. Mama responded with a forced "Thank you," followed by, "But what am I going to do with this fancy soup terrine?" She left it sitting on the table where Robert had put it, without even touching it. Later, when Robert left the room, she picked it up, turned it over, and looked at the bottom of it. "That's a Rosenthal," she gasped, looking at Papa, then at me. China from Rosenthal was some of the most prized china in all of Europe. "How did he get his hands on a piece like this? He must have stolen it." She picked up my figurine. "And this is a Meissen." This, too, was priceless.

Many goods being traded on the black market these days came from homes and apartments seized to house American troops. Neighbors down the street from us, who had to give up their apartments to the Amis reported that everything they had to leave behind had disappeared, including their furniture, pilfered by GIs

165

quartered there. These items showed up in some GI's girlfriends' home, others on the black market.

When Robert reentered the kitchen, Mama restrained herself and asked him as casually as she could muster, "Where did you get this terrine and this figurine?"

"A German lady gave it to me for doing her a little favor."

"Is that so? That must have been some favor you did for her." Irony colored her every word.

"Not really. It was just standing around, and in her way, she said. Why? Don't you like it?" Robert did not seem to have a clue as to the value of these pieces.

"Are you sure this hasn't been stolen? Nobody just gives you a piece like this for a little favor."

By now, I knew Robert well enough to read his face. Whenever he lied, he assumed a blank expression, like a brainless idiot. My doubting stares made him squirm and angry.

"God damn it! Quit looking at me as if I'm some kind of thief." In a fit of temper, he flung the cigarette lighter that was in his hand across the room. It bounced and hit the picture of my brother hanging on the wall behind my father's chair, breaking the glass. Mama flew into a full-blown rage.

"Get out of my house!" she screamed at him. "And take that stolen stuff with you."

"I've had it. I've had it. I'm leaving!" Robert gnashed through his teeth.

Turning on me, Mama fumed, "I can't understand what you see in this rogue. How did you ever get mixed up with him? He is no good."

"Mama...Mama! Please!" I tried to stem her outburst, looking at Papa for help. But as usual, he stayed out of the conflict. He picked up the shattered picture, moved the chair and table out of the way, and turned to Mama. "Get me the dustpan and a broom." That distracted her momentarily, long enough for Robert to grab his cigarettes and the terrine, and retreat to my room.

"I've had enough," he said. "You have got to find another place. I'm not coming back here."

"And just where am I supposed to go? There is no other place." My voice drowned in tears. I did not know whom I hated more at this moment, my mother or Robert. My mother was right, of course. I should have never gotten involved with Robert, but what was I supposed to do? Had I screamed and made a scene that night at the hotel in Stuttgart, I would be in jail now, and so would be the Dubskys. In the end, the outcome could have been even worse, and my mother would have ranted, "How can you do this to us? Who is going to support you?" Suddenly it dawned on me that I had never had anyone to lean on.

Since early childhood, I shouldered my family's struggles. We were poor because I did not practice enough; because I was too shy to sidle up to celebrities; or because I was too careless, got hurt and was unable to perform when we so desperately needed the money. When Robert said, "I stand by you," when I thought that I was pregnant, these were words I wished I had heard my parents say to me. It may have changed everything.

Mama still ranted on in the kitchen when the doorbell rang. Though the door to my room was closed, I could tell by the shuffle of Papa's pantoffles that it was he who opened the door.

"Hello!" I heard a high-pitched, cheery voice twitter. "Do you remember me? I am Ulla. Mitzi and I..."

"Oh! Of course, I remember. Ulla from Berlin. You and Mitzi danced together. Come on in," my father said. Opening my door, he announced, "You have company."

I stepped out into the hallway, where Mama and Ulla shook hands.

"Well! Greetings!" I said. "That's a surprise."

"I told you we would see each other again." Ulla grinned. Then she saw my bulging belly and gasped, "Oh, my! That explains why I haven't seen you around, dancing somewhere."

"Come on in and meet my fiancé." I ushered her into my room. Mama let out a puff of air in disgust, and cast a downward glance in the direction of my room and Robert, then retreated to the kitchen.

"This is Robert. Robert this is Ulla," I introduced them. Ulla looked slim and pretty, with her face made up and her fingernails painted. I could not help but notice how Robert's eyes traced every curve and inch of her. She, in turn, sized up Robert.

"Would you like some tea? All I have is peppermint, and some bread and jelly," I offered.

"Oh, that would be nice," she answered sweetly, throwing a demure glance at Robert. He invited her to sit down on my daybed, while I went to the kitchen to fix tea, bread and jelly. Neither Mama nor Papa said a word. When I returned to my room with the tea and jellied bread, I found Robert sitting beside Ulla, engaged in cozy conversation.

Though Ulla and I had danced in the same company together for over two years, we had been anything but friends. Still, we went through a lot together, and often had to depend on one another for survival, especially during six months on the Russian front. It was not something one easily forgets.

"So! How are you and Perry making out? Are you performing in Munich right now?" I inquired.

"No. Perry and I divorced. Right now, I'm looking for a job. I'm staying with a friend." Turning to Robert, she asked, "You wouldn't know where I could find a job...I would and could do just about anything."

"Anything?" Robert reiterated, chuckling and flashing his eyebrows. "I have to go to the caserne in a little while. I can ask around."

"Oh, I would be so grateful." She looked up at him from under her long, blackened eyelashes. The red of her lips and rouged cheeks emphasized the green of her eyes, turning them into marbles of jade.

"Will you be here when I get back?" Robert asked.

"I can be back tomorrow," she blinked and looked at me. "If that's all right with you, Mitzi."

"I'll be here," I said.

Finishing their tea, Robert and Ulla left together.

I cleared the table, listening to warnings of my inner voice. If the opportunity presented itself, I knew that either one would betray me. It no longer mattered. I was beyond hurt, but had to think of my child. How would I feed it? I witnessed mothers at the dairy beg and cry for milk for their hungry infants. Baby formula was as scarce as everything else, and I had yet to find even bottles and nipples.

Robert came back that same evening, ignoring my mother's demands to stay away. I rejected his advances and refused to bed with him, spending the night on a cot in a storage area. This infuriated him, though I had told him that I was simply following doctor's orders.

The next afternoon, Ulla showed up again. I had to help my mother with our monthly laundry and had to leave Ulla for longer periods in Robert's company. Later, as I dished up Spam and sardines that Robert had brought with him, I noticed the gold watch Ulla was wearing. "That looks exactly like the watch Robert gave me," I commented, surprised. "Where did you get it?"

Ulla looked discomfited at Robert. On a hunch, I looked into my jewelry box where I had put my watch earlier. It was gone.

"This *is* my watch," I gasped, and looked questioningly at Robert. He squirmed.

"Oh, I just gave it to her to wear," he said. "I meant to get you a new and nicer one anyway."

An icy calm came over me. Turning to Ulla, I demanded, "Take it off." She avoided my gaze, but complied. I grabbed their coats in the hallway and threw them at their feet. "You had better leave. Now! Both of you."

"You don't understand," Robert sputtered.

"Leave," I repeated, holding the door open for them. "And don't forget your duffel bag." I reminded Robert. He cursed under his breath and slipped into his coat.

"And here...you can take this with you, too," I added, and gave him back his ring.

Chapter 13

The War Within

𝕽obert came back that evening, apologizing to my parents, especially to my mother, saying that he had felt sorry for Ulla and was only trying to make her feel better. I refused to see him or talk to him. Mama jumped on me, "What do you mean, turning him away, now that you are about to have his child?"

"Mama!" I stared at her in disbelief. "It was you who ordered him out of your house long before I did. Not a day went by that you didn't nag me to get rid of him. Now, that you got your wish, you are having a fit. Is there anyway to please you?" Exasperated, I threw my arms up in the air. "Tell me, what in hell do you want me to do?"

"You should have asked me that before you got yourself pregnant."

"Sometimes I think that I'm just good enough to bring home food and money. After that, I am on my own. Is that it?" I snapped back. There! I finally spit out what had been festering inside me for a long time.

My mother gasped. When she found her breath again, she screamed, "You ungrateful child, you..." followed by a litany of sacrifices she had made in my behalf.

I stomped out of the house. The weather was as stormy outside as inside. A neighbor, Frau Pinzack, saw me standing in the rain, sobbing, and asked me to come in. "There...there," she said. Her voice was full of compassion. "Come sit down and relax a while. Getting so upset is not good for the baby." She pulled a kitchen chair out for me to sit down and poured me a cup of lukewarm tea from a ceramic pitcher. Her soft, sympathetic tone did not stop my tears, but eased the anger-caused spasms in my stomach.

I had always liked that woman, a war widow who had also lost her only two sons. She exuded an air of dignity, never seemed to gossip, was friendly, but kept to herself. Besides, she was one of few women not involved in altercations with my mother.

Setting the cup of tea in front of me, she sat down across from me. Folding her hands and resting her arms on the table, she looked at me and said, "So, how much longer before the big event?"

"Around the first of December."

"An early Christmas present then," she said and smiled.

It was meant to cheer me up, but at that moment I saw no light, no hope, only darkness looming. "How will I manage? Where will I go? How will I and my baby survive?" These thoughts triggered suffocating panic. I knew of no one who could or would take me in.

"Both of my boys were born in December," she reminisced, then added, barely audible, "and both died in December, at Stalingrad." She glanced at some photos of them hanging on the wall. How healthy, young and handsome they looked in their *Luftwaffe* uniforms.

"My brother died New Year's Eve, also killed at Stalingrad," I told her. We shared our common pain in a long silence. A wall clock ticked away the seconds. Tick...tack...tick...tack. It was the only sound in the room.

"I wish I were dead, too," I finally said, sobbing anew.

"Oh, don't say that. You have so much to live for...with a baby coming. The worst...the war is behind us. Maybe life will get better again. Tomorrow is a new day and you will see things differently."

I would have liked to talk my troubles out, but was ashamed to. At that moment, I was so angry at my mother that I would have said things I later might regret. Instead, we talked about the weather, what a cold and rainy summer it had been.

"I am convinced that all the bombings and fires had something to do with the changes in the weather," Frau Pinzack reasoned. "I can't remember ever having experienced such a wet and cold September. This certainly is not Octoberfest weather."

"Octoberfest...!" It was the farthest from my mind. But had it not been for the war, this would have been the time of year, late September, when it was held.

The Octoberfest was Munich's biggest fall festival— a medley of parades, oompah music, beer tents, rides and hawkers—a revelry that lasted two weeks, attracting visitors from near and far. It was held on a large meadow in the heart of the city at the foot of Munich's patron saint, a huge statue of Bavaria.

Instead of evoking happy memories, as Frau Pinzack may have hoped, in my present state of mind I remembered only what I had been denied; watching other children having fun on rides, licking ice cream, munching on giant pretzels and sausages, and walking off with balloons, kewpie dolls and other trinkets. My parents seldom had a penny to spare to let me go on a ride, or buy me a treat. They had to rob my piggy bank just to pay for the tram fare to get to the place. "When I grow up," I used to tell myself, "I'll get on every ride there is, see everything there is to see, and stuff myself with all this tempting food." That dream, too, fell victim to the war. I could not stop crying.

I finished my tea and rose to my feet. "Thank you. I guess I had better head for home."

Frau Pinzack saw me to the door. "Whatever happens, it's God's will. I'll say a prayer for you."

Night had settled on the city. The streets were dark except for the soft glow from a window here and there. It had quit raining. A jeep stood parked in front of our unit, which meant that Robert was still there, waiting for me. I decided to go for a walk, taking back roads and alleys. Frau Pinzack's parting words still rang in my ear. "It's God's will." At times, when I hit such awful lows, I wished with all my heart that I could still believe; that I could, like so many faithful, lean on God for comfort and for help. But, how could I? I saw no evidence of a God who cared. "God's will?" I mumbled to myself. "The war? The suffering? The heartache? Millions killed; entire families wiped out? God's will?"

I remembered the many believers crowding into churches at the first sound of the air raid sirens, praying and trusting that God would protect them while in His house. God's houses crumbled and the worshippers in it perished just as randomly as all others. Nowhere did I see evidence of a divine intervention or selection. I felt betrayed.

Though I no longer believed in this God the churches taught, I still prayed. Deep within my being, I felt connected to something larger than this life on earth, and sent my soundless cries out into the darkness of the universe. "Help me...help me."

Realizing that I could not stay out all night, I returned home. The jeep was gone. Papa let me in and I went to my room. Not a word was spoken. I found a note from Robert on the table, in which he begged my forgiveness, saying that he was trying to get a transfer to Munich to be with me for the birth of our child. Enclosed were two dollars.

During the next few days, I consulted with a midwife, recommended by neighbors. She felt my stomach, listened to the baby's heartbeat, and measured my pelvis with what looked like gigantic pinchers. "You had better see a doctor," she ultimately recommended. "You may need a cesarean section to deliver the baby. I definitely would not advise you to have the baby at home."

Worried, I followed her recommendation and saw a doctor who made arrangements with a birthing clinic run by the Catholic Church. Meanwhile, my friend Hanni, neighbors and other friends helped me find the barest necessities—a baby bottle, talcum powder, and a few odds and ends of baby clothes.

The relationship with my parents remained frosty and tense. We hardly spoke to one another. By now, my stomach was so large that I was mostly housebound, spending my days cutting and sewing old sheets into little shirts and diapers and knitting old wool remnants into a baby bonnet and booties. I also read a lot and practiced on the piano.

The due date came and went, but the doctor did not seem alarmed. Because of widespread starvation, he had seen pregnancies extend a month or more beyond the normal time. Finally, on December 13, early in the morning, I woke up to acute stomach cramps. It was time. I got up, got dressed, and awakened my father. "I think I have to go to the hospital."

Arrangements had been made earlier with a neighbor who had a car and driving permit to take me to the clinic. A small suitcase with everything I needed was packed and ready. I was anxious. My father went to notify the neighbor.

Around nine o'clock in the morning, I arrived at the clinic and was assigned a bed in a room with four beds on the ground floor. The building was unheated. Neither my father nor my mother had come with me. By now, my pains came stronger and in shorter intervals. Without getting undressed, I stretched out on the bed and pulled the covers over me but could not stop shivering. Not having the slightest idea what to expect, I was even more scared than I was cold. Nobody had ever explained anything about the process of giving birth.

A nurse in a nun's habit came into the room with forms for me to fill out. Handing them back, I felt embarrassed having had to state that I was not legally married and that my child was by an American GI. She then made me change into my nightshirt and sent me to the fourth floor, to the birthing station. I had no robe but wore my coat. Though the building had an elevator, it was out of order and I had to climb three flights of stairs, pausing and doubling over with each contraction. Sweat pearled on my forehead.

When I reached the top, I joined several women in various stages of labor, waiting to see the doctor. Some paced the floor; one was on her knees, praying, screaming and wailing; another sat silent and morose on a bench that lined the hallway. One after the other was called into the doctor's examining room, then either sent back to her room or shown to her birthing bed. When it was my turn, the doctor asked a few questions about the frequency of my contractions, examined me briefly, and sent me back to my room.

"How much longer, Herr Doctor?" I asked.

"First child? Not before this evening," he said.

"Holy Mother Mary!" I said to myself. "Give me strength. I am not going to last; I am not going to be able to stand this pain for seven or eight more hours." Holding on to the railing with both hands, I dragged myself down those three flights of stairs and into my room, crying.

I was alone and scared, without a soul to reassure and comfort me. How could my parents be so cruel to forsake me at this hour? There was no one in the room with me. The other beds stood empty.

The contractions became so severe and frequent that I called the nurse.

"Is this your first baby?" she asked. I nodded. "Well, then you have some time to go. First babies always take longer."

I waited until she had left, grabbed my coat and headed for the stairs. Bathed in sweat now, I made it to the top and cried out in panic, "My baby is coming...I know it's coming," to the first person I saw. She was a midwife, sitting in a closet-like cubicle knitting on a sock. Without stopping her knitting she looked up, asked me a few questions and told me to go back to my room.

"I can't stand this pain any longer. It doesn't stop at all anymore. Do something. Please do something," I begged.

"If you can't stand it, you shouldn't have gotten yourself pregnant," she replied.

I had a sudden urge to go to the toilet. Something burst. I heard a splash and felt momentary relief as if I had just dropped a hundred pounds. Then, sudden panic. Oh, my God! My baby had slipped out and I flushed it down the toilet. "Help...help!" I ran out to the midwife, screaming, "I think I lost my baby!"

I heard laughter.

"Didn't I tell you to go back down to your room?" the midwife admonished me. "Your water broke. That's all. No need to get hysterical."

At that instant, I let out such a grunt that the midwife dropped her knitting, jumped out of her chair, grabbed a smock and pulled me on to a bed, urging, "Don't push, don't push." But I could not help it, I grunted and pushed. In a bed next to mine lay a woman in labor screaming the entire time. "For God's sake, shut up," the midwife yelled at her as she dashed back and forth, collecting towels and cotton and whatever else she needed. Total chaos.

My baby was born before the midwife had been able to slip into the second sleeve of her smock. It was a girl with features undeniably those of her father's, but she was perfect.

"A girl." My wish had come true. Pleased but exhausted I sank back on the bed.

The midwife's demeanor was apologetic now. "Who would have thought that a first baby could come so quickly." She grumbled that the bath water, heating on a spirit burner, had not even had time to get warm. After she weighed and bathed the baby, she handed her to me, wrapped in a sheet.

"Have you selected a name for the baby?"

"Her name is Helene Luzia." Helene was my mother's favorite niece who had died at the age of sixteen in the US during the world's worst flu epidemic in 1908. Luzia was simply a name I liked.

The midwife took the baby's footprints and started filling out the birth certificate

"Father?"

"Robert M. H..., Corporal, United States Army."

"Oh...! And where is he? Gone, of course. They make babies and then they leave."

"He is stationed in Bremen. He'll be back soon:"

I tried to ignore the sarcasm in her voice and focused on my baby, my very own, my flesh and blood. A down of dark, fine hair covered her head. Her jerky little hands balled into fists, trying to find her mouth. An indescribable feeling of love and devotion welled up inside me, moving me to tears.

A nun came to get the baby; another helped me down the stairs, into my room and into bed. I gave them the clothes I had brought along for Luzi. The next time I saw my little girl, she was diapered and dressed in one of the little shirts I had sewn. And she was hungry. A nun brought her every four hours to let her nurse, then took her back to the nursery.

On the third day in the hospital, I had a visitor. It was Adele, one of my mother's long time friends.

"I saw your folks yesterday. They said you were in here having the baby. How did it go?"

When I told her how I panicked, thinking I had flushed the baby down the toilet, she laughed until she cried.

"Well? What is it?" she asked after she regained her composure.

"It's a girl."

"Just what you wanted, isn't it? Did you name her yet?"

"Her name is Helene Luzia."

"Can I see her?"

I sat up, put my slippers on and walked with her to the nursery. A nurse brought little Luzi to the window. Her wrinkled face had smoothened and turned rosy.

"Oh, she is so cute," Adele cooed. "Have your folks seen her yet?"

"No."

"They haven't come to see you?"

"No."

I did not let on how deeply hurt I was by my parents' absence.

"I'll bet when they see her, they'll fall in love with her."

During my five days in the hospital, a priest visited me every day, urging me to get the baby baptized. "If something should happen to her, you would want her to go to heaven, don't you?" He preached to me about the inherited sins of a newborn, that only baptism could remove.

I did not want to argue with the priest, who was still a figure of respect for me, but I resisted his pressure. I wanted Luzi to find her own faith some day.

The day of my release—I was dressed and had my suitcase packed already—I walked to the nursery to get my little girl. The door was ajar and I quietly opened it a little more to see if I could spot a nurse. What I saw was a nun sitting on the priest's lap. Momentarily stunned, I discretely retreated to my room. It should not have surprised me. It was widely known and snickered about that even bishops and cardinals had secret liaisons. Beneath the habit and the cloth of respectability and godliness beat the heart of a human being with all its strengths and weaknesses. It just confirmed what I had suspected already years ago, that they are no holier than the rest of us.

The hospital helped me hire a taxi. I bundled Luzi in a crocheted blanket and put a bonnet on her sweet little head. She looked so delicate that I was afraid to handle and hurt her.

Though it was the middle of December, it had not snowed recently, nor was it extremely cold that day. As the taxi bounced along rough, cobbled streets, the desolated city rolled by like a black and white movie clip. Up a long hill we followed a huffing-puffing, smoke-belching slow truck fueled by wood chips. The impatient taxi driver stepped on the gas to get around it and almost collided with an army truck coming the other way. His swerving tossed me from side to side with Luzi in my arms, but she slept through it all.

As the taxi turned into the street where I lived, my heart thumped like a kettledrum. I feared what I had to face next. The driver stopped in front of our unit and helped me inside, carrying my suitcase. Hearing me enter the apartment, my father came out of the kitchen to investigate. When he saw me, he retreated and shut the kitchen door again. I went to my room, put the baby onto my daybed, tipped the driver, and closed the door. This was my home, yet I felt like a stranger among strangers.

Chapter 14

A Reason for Living

The next weeks revealed just how little I knew about caring for an infant. Still so hurt by my parents' attitude—we had not spoken more than a few words since I came home—I stubbornly refused to ask for their help. Already by the end of the first day, I had run out of clean diapers and clothes for the baby. Diapers made from old, threadbare bed sheets absorbed very little and I had no rubber panties to slip over them. When the baby wet, she wet everything. This was December. Though I immediately rinsed everything and hung it up to dry, outside, the laundry froze stiff; inside, in our unheated bathroom, it stayed wet for days. I hung a few items on the guardrail in front of the oven door during cooking time. This was also the only time when the kitchen and the water in the cistern were warm enough to bathe the newborn. So afraid that I might hurt my tiny infant daughter, I handled her so gingerly that, during her first bath in a small, galvanized washtub, she slipped out of my hands and her face went momentarily under water. I panicked, thinking I had drowned her, but she did not even cry.

Watching my clumsy struggles from the sidelines, my mother grew more frustrated by the minute until she could stand it no longer and pitched in. So did my father. He strung a line above the kitchen stove where I could hang the laundry.

The ice was melting. Adele, my mother's friend, was right. It did not take long before Luzi became the center of my parents' lives.

Another Christmas and New Year had come and gone, my baby's first. Two-and-a-half years after the war, it had been bleaker than all others, without a tree, without presents. I did not care. My only concern was for my child to survive the winter. I traded away much of what Robert had given me, and with the occasional dollars he sent I bought wood and coal to take the chill out of my room.

After weeks of nursing my child, my breasts became sore, then raw, and then bloody. I saw the doctor who advised me to get a pump. A pump? Where would I get a pump? The doctor did not know. "Ask around," he said. Once again, my father hopped on his bike and made the rounds of his former clients. He had found me silver sandals for the stage; maybe he could find me a pump.

Knocking on many doors, my father finally did come home with a pump, but it was already too late. I drew mostly blood and had to put little Luzi on a powder and water formula the doctor was able to get for me. We had no milk. The doctor urged me to expose her as much as possible to fresh air and sunlight to prevent a vitamin deficiency. Following his recommendations, I bedded Luzi in her carriage and, whenever the sun peeked out, I walked up and down the snow and ice covered sidewalks on the sunny side of Nauplia

Strasse, until I thought my toes would fall off from frost-bite.

While out walking, I regularly encountered another young mother doing the same. We exchanged smiles, then a greeting, until one day we stopped to chat. Her child, a boy, was six months older than Luzi, wearing a cute little hooded snowsuit in light blue. I commented on it, since I had never seen anything like it.

"His grandmother sent it from America. The boy's father is an American," she explained.

We introduced ourselves—her name was Jutta—and because we shared common ground, connected quickly.

Jutta's fiancé had been discharged from the army and gone home, but had promised to send for her and their son as soon as the paperwork came through. He and his parents regularly sent money and whatever else she needed. "They are so very good to me," she acknowledged thankfully.

Indeed, her little boy had everything, from soft, absorbent diapers and cuddly blue blankets to cute outfits and toys. When I told her about my plight, that I did not even have rubber panties and barely enough diapers and clothes for my baby, she offered to loan me some items her little boy had outgrown. I was grateful beyond words.

Jutta and I became friends. We shared notes. She lived with her mother in a two-room unit not far from me. There were just the two of them. She never mentioned her father or other family members, and I knew better than to ask. The violence of the war had affected just about everyone. Wounds were often still too fresh, and for many, it was still too painful to talk about what had happened to them or their kin. We focused on the present and our children. She told me that she had met her fiancé in late summer of 1946, while sunbathing with friends at the shores of the Isar River. Like so many GIs, he was homesick and looked for a substitute family. He started visiting her.

"He is a nice guy. I liked him from the start. My mother thinks he would make a better husband than most German men because he can fix just about everything around the house," Jutta chuckled. She seemed content and happy.

I shied away from telling her about my situation, fearing that the dam might break that was holding back my pain, my fears and anger.

◆   ◆   ◆

Luzi was six weeks old when Robert first saw her. Seeing father and child together, everyone commented on their strong resemblance. Robert seemed flattered.

He had come to Munich to audition for an announcer's job at the American radio station. While he was in town, he filed papers with the American authorities, declaring that he was Luzi's father, thus making her automatically a US citizen. He thought that this would help speed up the authorization to get married and the process of obtaining an immigration visa for me.

Robert's stay was short and limited to only brief visits.

My attitude toward him had softened. At least Robert proved willing to assume the responsibility of fathering a child. Many American GIs did not. They disappeared, never to be heard from again, often encouraged and supported by their superiors.

While in town, Robert had pictures taken of Luzi and me to send home to his parents who still had not even acknowledged us. For the photo session, I wore the dress he had bought for me from an American nurse when I was pregnant.

Not long after Robert's audition, he got his transfer and became an announcer on the Munich AFN station. But as soon as he appeared permanently on the scene again, trouble at home erupted anew. His annoying habits of coughing and spitting into his cup, or helping himself without asking to the last morsel of food that we had in the house infuriated my mother. The situation became so intolerable that I had to move out.

Robert bribed German officials to assign me a room in a once luxury apartment house that had at least structurally survived the war. I shared the facilities with several other tenants, people from a list of Nazi victims. It was here that I became reunited with Angi, a young woman I had befriended while working at the Agfa factory toward the end of the war.

Angi was from Posnan, Poland. Nazi's had arrested and shipped her to Germany, forcing her to work at the Agfa, just like me. We had worked side by side, but because she was a prisoner, we were strictly forbidden to talk to one another. Ignoring these stupid rules, we engaged in whispered conversations. When I could, I slipped her food—half of my jelly sandwich, or an apple, or whatever I could spare. We Germans were starving, but prisoners even more so.

In charge of our workstation was a middle-aged woman, a fanatic devotee of Hitler, who turned us in to a male supervisor every time she caught us talking. The supervisor, a nice older fellow, gave us a warning and left it at that. Then one day, my parents and I were startled out of bed at five o'clock in the morning by the persistent ringing of the doorbell.

"It's the Gestapo...it's the Gestapo," my mother gasped. My father opened the door and in stormed two men in black uniform asking for me. They ordered my parents into the kitchen and started to search our apartment. I was still in bed, and remained there as they barged into my room. "Where is Angi. Where have you hidden her?" they asked in a threatening tone.

"Angi who? Oh...I don't know. How would I know where Angi is?" I answered, dumbfounded.

"You were seen talking to her at the factory."

"So? Yes, I talked to her."

The men searched through everything. They looked in my wardrobe, behind my wardrobe, under the bed, behind my bed, in my drawers. "Where is she? Do you know where is she?"

Still in bed, still in my nightgown, I watched them and started to laugh. I thought it was hilarious for them to search for Angi in my chest drawers.

"Maybe I have hidden her under my blankets," I mocked and lifted them up. "And don't forget to look in the table drawer."

For a moment, both men paused and stared at me befuddled. It seemed as if they had never been laughed at before. Shortly thereafter they left.

Mocking them was not an act of defiance, bravery or foolishness. It was calculated. "Never run when confronted by a vicious dog. Never show your fear when a bully comes at you." These lessons I had learned growing up.

When my parents heard the door shut behind the Gestapo, they charged out of the kitchen, visibly shaken, but glad to see that they had not taken me away. I was still laughing.

"How can you laugh? We thought they were going to take you away," my mother fretted. "What were they searching for?"

I told my parents about Angi, who apparently had escaped. "Good for her!" I cheered.

"Don't press your luck," my parents warned. "They don't bother making arrests anymore, they just shoot the people now."

187

The following day I was called into the factory director's office. The director, a short, bald-headed older man who must have had still plenty to eat because he was round as a barrel, stood in front of his massive desk, flanked by the two Gestapo men and the woman snitch from my workstation.

"She is the one," the woman screeched and pointed at me the moment I walked through the door. "I saw them whispering the day before that Polack disappeared."

One of the men slapped a braided leather club against his thigh.

"You admit that you have been talking to this prisoner, in spite that it is forbidden?" he started the interrogation.

"Yes."

"What did you talk about?"

"About Poznan," I answered, thinking how stupid of them, as if I would tell them anything even if I had known about Angi's plans.

"What's your interest in Poznan?"

"I have been in Poznan, danced before the German Military High Command...just before I left for the Russian Front." Speculatively and intentionally, I volunteered this extra information. Having served six months on the Russian front was a trump card. It demanded respect and leniency even from the Gestapo.

"Have you ever been on the Russian front?" I hastened to add.

Throwing this question at them had the calculated effect. I had seen this strategy being used quite successfully by veterans on overbearing, arrogant bureaucrats and officials. For men, not having been on the Russian front was like a brand of cowardliness. It worked.

The interrogation continued, but not quite as harshly. The snitch did not like the way it was going and constantly interjected, "I saw her give that Polack an apple...She was always giving her something...I just knew they were plotting something."

"From what I saw in your lunch bucket, you could have shared a lot more," I needled her. "Where did you got the ham, the butter and the eggs? You didn't get them with your ration tickets." The snitch's face turned red. Her eyes darted nervously back and forth between the Gestapo and the director. I had her cornered.

The Gestapo told her to shut up and dismissed her. While this was going on, I noticed that the director covered his face with a handkerchief to hide a chuckle. Once the snitch was out of the room, the director informed the Gestapo that there was not a worker in his factory that this sour old prune had not turned in for one thing or another. I was released and sent back to work. The snitch, complaining that her patriotism had been betrayed, shriveled into silence.

Already before this incident, I had to be transferred on doctor's orders to a different department at the factory. The monotonous, repetitive up-and-down motion, working a lever on a rivet press all day long, had caused me to develop a stomach ulcer. Making it worse was that the snitch constantly exceeded our quota, putting the pressure on all of us who worked these presses to match it.

I was glad to be transferred to the watchmaker's department, located just across the aisle from where I had worked before. There I learned to assemble and adjust timing devices for bombs. This department had only one other woman, the rest were men—former jewelers and watchmakers.

I had it made. Being young and female, I became a sort of pet of the department. The men did most of the work for me, while I entertained everybody with my little shenanigans, targeting people like the snitch and our grouchy supervisor. When my co-workers found out that I could lay cards, I had no time left at all to do my job. One after another wanted me to do a reading for them. I had a waiting list a mile long, and they brought me food, vegetables and fruit from their gardens, or offered to pay me in silver coins. For most of each day, I was gone from my post, secretly meeting in the washroom, or at lunch. The department supervisor scratched his head when I delivered my quota at the end of each day. I could tell what he was thinking. "How does she do that? I never see her do any work." But as long as I could deliver, he did not care.

For a while, I thought this was great, getting paid for laying cards and having fun, until I realized that this was not just an entertaining game anymore. My frivolous predictions became someone's desperate last straw, their last glimmer of hope. Just about everybody had men on the front, or family members in some of the heavily bombed cities who were missing. I read the agony in their faces over not knowing if they were dead or alive, or had been taken prisoner. What had started out as fun suddenly turned into a gut-wrenching nightmare for me. "Look, I don't know any more than you do," I tried to tell them. "This is a game. I can't see into the future." They did not care. They were so desperate that even a bright lie was better than the dark unknown.

I wrestled with my conscience. What is the right thing to do? Take their last straw of hope, or keep on lying to calm their fears?

◆　◆　◆

Angi and I recalled those days at the Agfa over a cup of tea. I was curious to find out how she was able to escape.

190

"I'd made friends with one of the night guards patrolling the factory and the labor camp," she explained, "and during one of the terrible air raids, he used the confusion to let me out. He lent me his bike and told me where to go and stay. Months later, the war was over and here I am."

"Are you planning to return to Poznan now, to your family?" I asked.

"No. How can I go home? Poznan is under the Russians now. I'd be worse off than under the Nazis," she replied, shrinking back with horror.

Her reaction was that of most of the people from Eastern Europe that had worked in labor camps. The majority did not want to go home and live under Russian rule. However, Americans had an agreement with the Russian government to repatriate them. And once again, these people had no choice. As before, they were carted away in cattle cars and delivered into the hands of oppressors by another name. Angi was lucky. She had found a job with the Americans as an interpreter, since she spoke Polish, German and English.

"Do you know if your family has survived?"

Angi shook her head and drew a deep breath. "I am trying to find out through the Red Cross."

For many families everywhere, it would be a long, drawn-out heartache to find one another and get back together, with many never learning the fate of their loved ones.

Angi's situation reminded me of a scene in a medieval glass factory in Russia my colleagues and I had been invited to visit. Fascinated, I watched the bare-chested, sweat-covered workers move in and out of the bright glow of a central furnace, extracting and working globs of molten glass. Suddenly, an old Russian woman rushed up and fell to her knees in front of me. With tears streaming down her hollow cheeks, she

kissed the hem of my skirt, then looked up at me, bab-
bling something in a language I did not understand. A
co-worker finally stepped forward to interpret. "Please
help me find my daughter. Find my daughter," she
pleaded. The co-worker briefly explained that most
young and able-bodied men and women had been
rounded up by the Nazi SS, loaded on a truck and taken
away to work in German factories, never to be seen or
heard from again.

I could not bring myself to share this story with Angi
or both of us would have cryed. But I wondered if this
Russian woman still lived and waited for her daughter,
and if her daughter would decide, like Angi, to stay in
Germany now.

My stay in the apartment house lasted two months.
My room was on the third floor. Without help, I could
not get the baby buggy up or down the stairs and was
very much housebound. Robert was often gone for
days, broadcasting from different locations—special
events such as sports competitions, ice shows or the
arrivals of celebrities. It was also still winter. Streets
and sidewalks were iced over with old snow. One day
my father came, telling me how much he and Mama
missed us, and to please come home again. I consented
quickly.

Whenever I was alone with my father, I was able to
talk to him about what was in my heart and mind. He
listened quietly when I told him that I was resolved to
marry Robert; that I did not want my child to go
through life labeled a bastard, and that he and Mama
simply had to accept that. Placing his hand over mine,
his gaze shifted from me to some distant place in time
and space. He breathed a deep sigh that said more
than words ever could. It spoke of concern, pain, love,
and the wisdom to know that even the best laid plans
only lead to uncertainty. The future had no roadmap.

Mitzi and baby (6 weeks old).

Luzi, 1 year old.

Luzi's father, Robert.

Dog Bearli and friend.

Everyone loves Luzi - Papa.

Robert.

Mama.

Neighbor, Frau Pinzack.

Chapter 15

The Process

Robert seemed quite proud and comfortable in his role as a father. He fed, burped and diapered little Luzi, carried her around when she cried, and insisted on pushing the baby carriage when we went for a walk. For Germans, it was an unusual sight for a man to push a baby carriage. German women smiled approvingly; German men accepted it as just another strange American custom.

Perhaps due to an American-fathered baby boom, the PX started to carry some baby food and baby items. Little Luzi seemed to thrive on Pablum, powdered milk, and pureed canned fruit. Weeks after Robert had sent photos of the baby and me home to his parents, a small package arrived with a pair of much appreciated rubber panties and soft, white overalls. This was their first acknowledgement of our existence.

Robert's applications for permission to marry, Luzi's American citizenship, and a visa for her and me to come to the U.S. inundated us with paperwork. All forms had to be filled out at least in triplicate. I had to furnish documents with authorized translations from German agencies that were scattered all over Munich. Biking from one end of the city to the other to gather them trimmed me down to a wiry one hundred pounds.

Weeks into this paper war, I received notice to report for a physical at an American army hospital in a former German *Kaserne* (barracks). Armed guards at the entrance to this cold, gloomy brick building checked my papers and ID before letting me pass. Heavy, ironclad doors led into a dingy stairway, where a GI clerk behind a makeshift desk stopped me.

"Here for a physical?"

I nodded.

"To your right," the clerk said, thumbing me in the direction of a yawning archway that loomed like the entrance to a dungeon. It opened onto a large space with the coldness of a warehouse. Cloth-covered, portable screens formed small cubicles along one wall. Several freestanding, curtained stalls down the middle divided the space in two. The rest was cluttered with boxes, equipment and handcarts with linens and supplies. Uniformed men, some wearing white coats, passed back and forth, paying no attention to me. Finally, one approached.

"You here for a physical?" He looked at the papers in my hand, told me to disrobe in one of the stalls, grabbed a bed sheet off one of the carts and handed it to me. "Here, you can put this around you."

A wave of anxiety dampened my skin. I wanted to run. It brought back memories of the humiliating experience at a German army hospital in Warsaw, when my colleagues and I had to line up like recruits, stark naked, for a physical before an all-male German staff. The setting and the lack of respect had outraged us. We had expected better treatment from our own. What could I expect from our occupiers? At least then, I was in the supportive company of my colleagues; now I was alone and scared to death.

As before, I capitulated to the powers in charge. Rebelling would have resulted in consequences far beyond the damage to my pride and dignity.

I undressed, wrapped the sheet around me and waited until I heard my name called. A doctor—I assumed he was because he had a stethoscope around his neck—directed me into one of the cubicles and onto an examining table. He turned on a bright light just above it, and in a detached manner proceeded to check the usual—blood pressure, heart rate, lungs, et cetera. It went fast.

"Good," I said to myself, "I'll be out of here in no time."

Just when I thought he was done with me, he bent my legs up, flipped the sheet back, and examined and swabbed my private parts. Never before had that been part of any physical examination. It plunged me into a state of quivering shock. I could not remember afterwards how I got off the table, why I had a bandage on my arm, and how I got back on the streetcar. I remember vaguely running into a group of women exiting from a paddy wagon as I dashed out of the building.

"Hey, watch where you're going!" The words rang in my ears, almost prophetic sounding: 'Watch where you're going.'

This experience thrust me into brooding silence. It spun around in my mind and burned in my cheeks, but I could not talk about it, at least not with my parents. Later, I mentioned it to Jutta.

"Hah! I know! That's why I am not in any hurry to get married and go to the States," she said. "I refuse to report every month for a VD check like a prostitute."

"A VD check? Every month?" I cringed. "How do you know that?"

"Just ask around among girls that want to marry a GI and go to the States."

Once again, I questioned with regret all the dumb decisions I had made that put me in this situation, from signing with the Dubskys to staying with Robert. Only when I held little Luzi in my arms did all self-disparaging doubts dissolve. She was a precious gift, a promise of a tomorrow, like new life greening on a field of death. And she was mine; my very own. I would not have had her had I made different choices, and who can say that they would have turned out any better. It renewed my determination to make the best of the situation and do whatever was necessary for my child's future, security and happiness.

My intentions were the best; they always had been. However, the times and situations I had to struggle through compared to fighting one's way through a jungle swamp. I thrashed on, trying to keep from being sucked under, from drowning in the muck of this bloody war and its aftermath. In the struggle to stay alive, I did not contemplate the future, or the dangers that might be lurking ahead. Life was lived from day to day. Only many years later, as I had to deal with the consequences of some of my disastrous decisions, did I wish I had zigged instead of zagged.

Luzi was six months old and sitting up. The dark fluff of hair she had at birth had lightened and grown into silken-soft blond curls. She was a doll and the joy of life for my parents and me. Hardly ever leaving her side was Bearli, a small dog a GI had left in our care and never reclaimed. The very first word Luzi uttered, when she was seven months old, was a raspy imitation of the word '*gut*', a word we kept using to coax her to eat. "This is *gut...gut* (good)." Now she used this technique on Bearli, feeding him whatever she did not like. "*Gut...gut,*" she mimicked, trying to get him to eat it.

Germany, at least the Western zones, showed slow signs of revival. In June 1948 the worthless Reichsmark was junked for the new Deutsch Mark (DM). Each person initially received 40.00 DM, and almost immediately varied goods and merchandise appeared in stores and streets of Munich. Unfortunately, most people could not afford to buy much. While the Reichsmark had been deflated at a rate of ten to one, the amount for rent, utilities and all other necessities had remained the same, and the masses were no better off than before.

Almost daily, foreign solicitors came to our door, offering everything from carpets, damask, wool suiting and fine crystal, to a variety of cookware. They spoke so little German that we could not find out where they or their goods came from. Much of what they offered was of good quality and cheap, but money was tight; besides, their merchandise could have been stolen.

My parents' metal-collection business took off, also. People without jobs and income scrounged through ruins and came with hand wagons full of twisted and scorched items from brass door handles, copper pots, cisterns, wiring, pewter, and silver, to iron girders, gates, and fences.

The Dollar was still in high demand and worth much more than its official exchange rate of four DM to one Dollar, and American cigarettes still commanded a premium price.

As the economy started to revive, so did some old German traits. During the hardest and most life-threatening times, people had bonded together in the common struggle to survive. The titled and the untitled had to depend on one another. Frau Dr. and Frau Director had greeted and chatted with Frau Meier, the *Putzfrau* (cleaning lady), when they met on the street. Suddenly, Frau Dr. and Frau Director did not seem to know Frau Meier anymore. Her friendly greeting, if acknowledged at all, earned a snobbish nod.

Occasionally, I ran into somebody from show business, with whom I had performed. I was delighted when I saw my friend Paula again. She was a singer and we had worked in many shows together. I had not seen her since I quit dancing. When we met on some street in Munich, we embraced, overjoyed to see each other again.

"What had happened to you?" she asked. "You suddenly vanished from the scene."

"It's a long story," I told her. "I'm a mother now."

"You got married?" she gasped.

"No. Not yet. I told you, it's a long story. But what about you? Are you still singing for the Amis?"

"Oh, no!" she answered with disdain. "I'm engaged to a professor from the university. I don't dare even mention that I sang for the Amis."

Both of us were pressed for time.

"We have to get together. I want to know all that's going on with you these days," I said.

"Yes," she agreed. "And I want to see your baby, too."

We decided that she would visit me at my house, and set a day and time.

Paula did come. Initially, we just relished being together again and filled in the lapses of time we had not seen each other.

"I would like to invite you to my wedding," she hesitated, "but my husband-to-be and his family don't want me to have any ties to people from show business. They think of them as circus people, Zigeuner (gypsies), people with low morals." Paula bowed her head. "If he knew that I came to see you, I think he would call off the wedding."

"Paula...! That's awful! Does that mean you can't perform and sing anymore?"

"I still can sing...at home...but not for an audience."

I wanted to ask why she married a man like that, who dictated what she could and could not do, and with whom she could be friends. I was appalled. Then I thought of my own situation. Who was I to talk!

When she left, we embraced. "I'll come again. He doesn't have to know."

The door shut behind her. I turned and leaned against it, trying to control my anger. "Damned these snobs," I gnashed through my teeth. I understood more and more why my father was the way he was. I knew I would be just like him. He never cowered or kissed anybody's boot. Neither would I.

From what Mama and some of our American friends had told me, America's system set no boundaries for the individual with initiative and a willingness to work hard. A common man could rise to become president. Harry S.Truman, once a farmer, now President of the United States, served as a glowing example. It sounded promising. Nothing, however, was said about the lot of women. I took my American Aunt Mathie as an example. She had visited us several times before the war with her common-law-husband, who was many years younger then she. Together, they owned a bakery in Philadelphia. Everyone thought that they were rich because they came with their car, and because Mathie wore chic clothes, fancy hats and shoes, and always smiled. Doormen at hotels bowed to her, waiters at restaurants hurried to serve her, store clerks vied to wait on her. She was treated royally, but never failed to share who she was and how she got what she had. "I work for what I have," she said and displayed her hands. "Look at them. These hands are not afraid to get dirty." Indeed, her hands were rough like the hands of a laborer, but she was proud of them. In spite of the fact that she had to work hard, she looked a decade younger than most of her contemporaries. She was confident, positive, and always in good spirits. When I compared her to my mother, I wanted to be like Mathie. "Maybe," I thought, "it has something to do with living in America."

Whenever I had qualms about following Robert to the States, I thought of Mathie. If she could make it, so could I.

On weekends, when Robert was on duty, I often got together with my friend Hanni, and we would sit and scour through the latest American magazines Robert had brought. In them, it pictured smiling housewives, looking like they had just stepped out of a beauty parlor, standing in built-in kitchens next to modern refrigerators, electric stoves, or washing machines. Or it showed happy couples driving down a scenic road in sleek looking convertibles. It showed neat bungalows with manicured front lawns where children frolicked—a picture perfect world, a world without want or worry.

While we salivated over every page, we also knew that this was not for real, not for us, and not unlike the fairy tales that used to spin in our heads.

"I just want my own room, or my own little apartment some day," Hanni sighed. Her brothers had finally come home from the war. One had been taken prisoner; the other had been badly wounded, lost a leg, and for months languished in German army hospitals. Now they shared the family's small apartment.

"Maybe you can come to the States," I said.

"I don't think so. I could never leave my family and my homeland," she answered.

When looking through the magazines, I searched for pictures of Nebraska, Robert's home state. I could not imagine myself in a place without mountains or forests, and already felt pangs of homesickness. I knew I would miss the Alps, and the woods, and the picturesque villages of Bavaria, as well as my parents and friends. But I also looked forward to be free—free of the chains of Germany's class-conscious society, and free of the shadows of war.

Chapter 16

Ironies of War

$\mathfrak{S}$hortly after the currency reform in 1948, the Iron Curtain came down, dividing Germany in two. Russia closed all borders to its occupied zone, as well as the Berlin Corridor. Barbed wire and machine-gun-brandishing Russian guards suddenly separated families and neighbors—husbands from wives, parents from children, children from their siblings. Not even the Western Allies, who won the war for Russia, were allowed into Berlin. For so many, war's tragedy played on.

The Iron Curtain also prevented any search for still missing family members, and it certainly foiled my attempts to reestablish contact with my friends and former colleagues.

Cut off from all life sustaining supplies, thousands of Berliners faced certain death. Just when they thought that nobody cared, Americans started the airlift. Pilots, once dropping megatons of deadly bombs on Berlin, now dropped food and life-saving supplies to the destitute, starving population below. It began with individual pilots dropping chocolate bars and chewing gum, attached to parachutes made from handkerchiefs, to waiting children below.

The Cold War had begun.

Once again, war clouds darkened on the political horizons. Newspapers headlined the daily tragedies of Easterners being shot by Russian guards while trying to escape to the West, often while American soldiers on the west side had to look helplessly on. Those lucky to survive the crossing told horror stories about conditions under the communists.

These developments had me question again the wisdom and policy of the Western Allies. So many lives could have been spared, had they come to an agreement with the German underground and military leaders who wanted to rid Germany of Hitler, and then march on against Stalin. By the way American soldiers talked, none of them seemed to realize or question that they were fighting side by side with, and aiding and abetting an equally evil tyrant—Stalin. They believed so wholeheartedly in their cause, and in the honorable intentions of their government. The few prophetic voices, such as General Patton's, drowned in a sea of controversy. Had it been left to him, history would have changed drastically. Later, his diaries and biographies would bear that out.

I often wondered what goes through the minds of generals and heads of state as they send thousands of men into battle and to their deaths. Bent over charts, they move little pegs and tiles around, no longer the toy soldiers from their boyhood, but representing hundreds or thousands of flesh and blood human beings. They don't see the carnage, they don't hear the screams of the wounded, they don't share the sorrow of mothers, fathers, sons and daughters. Insulated by their importance, they remain clean, warm, and safe, as they go on plotting their killing strategies.

Tensions between the East and West escalated. I noticed yet again a shift in political policies. The "hated land of the Huns and the Nazis," as Germany had been described in the press, quickly moved into the position of an ally. Germans wrung their hands, fearing that if the East and West declared war on one another, Germany would become the battleground again. Most people could not decide what was worse—another war, or falling under communist control.

Though Germany and the Allies had not yet signed a peace treaty, by late summer 1948 Konrad Adenauer became West Germany's first postwar president and Bonn its capital. Policies by the occupational forces toward Germans eased; thus sanctioning, and even encouraging friendly interaction between Germans and Americans. This promised to speed up the paperwork for many war brides, such as myself, to marry and follow their husbands to the United States.

Robert had settled into his job as radio disk jockey and did well. He had a rich and pleasant voice, excellent diction, and was in charge of daytime musical programs, including an hour of classical music. He actually liked classical music, from Bach to Beethoven and had always fancied to becoming an opera singer some day. I listened regularly to the AFN station. One time I asked Robert if he could play something from Richard Wagner, one of my favorite composers. I was shocked to learn that his music was banned in Germany. When I asked why, I was told because it was Hitler's music. If my memory serves me right, Richard Strauss also fell into disfavor. But we did hear again the works by Hindemith and other composers who had been banned by the Nazis. Among other banned pieces of music was a favorite Christmas carol of mine—*Hohe Nacht der Klaren Sterne.* Because it had always been played just before Joseph Goebbels' speech on Christmas Eve, I have not heard it again to this day.

The radio station broadcast from the Kaulbach villa, a palatial private residence once belonging to the great German painter Wilhelm von Kaulbach. It had survived the war and now housed Amis. Robert took me to some functions there and introduced me to his commander, Major Giagandit, as his fiancée.

The first time the major and I met, he sized me up, his eyes switching back and forth between Robert and me. Finally, he asked, "Do you love this guy?" I held his gaze, knowing what my answer should be—an enthusiastic "Yes." But, that important little word stuck in my throat. I just could not spit it out. Instead, I answered, "He is the father of my child." He flattened his chin and nodded thoughtfully.

"I blew it," I told myself. To get married, we needed his endorsement. Later, out of earshot of everyone, Robert exploded. "You embarrassed the shit out of me. He's never going to sign the papers now," he said, followed by a barrage of vulgar expletives. I let it run off me like water. Sticks and stones...he could curse all he wanted. I would have felt worse had I lied to the major.

The PX now offered incredible buys: fine china, wool blankets from Holland, watches from Switzerland, and cameras from the Agfa in Germany. Robert bought Leica and Retina cameras, a set of fine china, and luxurious, fluffy blankets to take back to the States. I often wondered, with dark suspicion, where he got the money. An incident at the radio station haunted me like an evil omen.

During a benefit drive at the radio station, a staff member interrupted the gathering, reporting a missing jar full of money that had been collected for the drive. Major Giagandit questioned his staff about the last time anyone had seen or handled it. Meanwhile, no one was allowed to leave the room and everyone had to submit to a search. Some bills had been marked since this was not the first time that money was missing. Robert was eager to help in the search; too eager, perhaps. I happened to look at him during the questioning. He wore that stupid expression again that he wore whenever I caught him in a lie.

Neither jar nor money could be found. Later, I asked Robert if he had any idea what could have happened to it. "How should I know? I didn't take it," he answered with a shrug. There it was again—that stupid look. In my heart I knew he was the thief, but had no proof.

Robert expected to return to the U.S. within six months, yet papers for our permission to marry still had not come through. Trying to trace them proved futile. We had to start all over. After the evasive answer I gave Major Giagandit, I had little hope that he would be helpful.

At this time, I lived mostly off my parents. Robert doled out a few dollars here and there, but I needed a steady income. I investigated the possibility of getting back into show business. Work for the Special Service had fallen off drastically. Shows came over from the States now. Many of my colleagues were out of work, and my agent Baretti was hurting, too. Only a few German theaters gradually reopened—mostly cabarets in holes in the wall.

Our singer-friend Sefi, who got me my first job after the war, performed in the *Platzl*, a famous Bavarian landmark located across from the *Hofbrauhaus* in downtown Munich. Both places had sustained heavy bomb damage, but the ground floor in each building was reclaimable. Through Sefi, I reconnected with a friend, Johann Roessler—humorist, author and screen-writer—who promised to put in a good word for me with the moguls in the movie industry.

If all should fail, my school friend Hanni said she could get me a job with an American family as a maid. "It's not bad. I get good pay and many other things," she said and showed me her wardrobe full of nice clothes and shoes.

Whatever it was that I had to do, I had to do. However, there was something about being a maid that caused me to bristle. At fourteen, serving my year in the Pflichtjahr as a maid for a pro Nazi officer's family, the lady of the house who came from a titled, well-to-do family predicted, "If you work hard, you may become a very good maid some day." She had assumed, because I came from poor parents, that this would be my highest attainable goal. Being my father's child, I rebelled.

"I feel born to higher purpose," I replied, nose in the air. And I still felt that way. I was going to defy this damned class system, which already showed strong signs of revival.

Luzi, in the meantime, had taken her first steps and started to walk and talk. Soft blond curls framed her face, grown long enough to hold a pretty bow. She was the darling of the neighborhood. Older children begged me to let them play with her, or to take her for a walk. *Oma*, my mother, took her shopping. *Opa*, my father, scavenged a small basket-seat to attach in front of his on his bicycle bar and took her for rides. He also found her a high chair with potty, so we could begin her potty training. With winter approaching, it was crucial to reduce the daily laundry.

Luzi was a good baby, cranky only when she was tired. People commented how clean and cared-for she looked. She appeared healthy, and from all indications, she was smart, too. I was concerned, however, about her eyes. When she became tired, one eye turned inward, making her appear cross-eyed. I asked our doctor what I should do. "Don't worry," she said. "She'll grow out of it. It's only a weak muscle."

I took no chances. Having learned that carrot juice contained vitamins that helped strengthen the eyes, I grated and squeezed one daily and spooned Luzi the juice. She liked it. I also tried to give her cod-liver oil, but could not get her to swallow it.

"Do as we did with you," my parents suggested. "Tell her it's beer."

My father once dipped Luzi's pacifier into his beer and gave it to her. From then on, whenever she saw us drink it, she reached out with both of her little hands, begging "Beer...beer." We let her have a little foam.

"A genuine *Muenchener Kindl*," my parents noted with pride. To Bavarians, beer was a national beverage, like wine was to the French. Not to like it, would have seemed strange.

Nearing the Christmas season, Robert received another small package from his folks. In it was a cute little pinafore dress and hat for Luzi. The color matched her blue eyes, but the dress was still too big on her. The package also contained a Christmas card addressed to me saying that they enjoyed the pictures Robert had sent of us. This was the first direct connection between his parents and me.

Luzi celebrated her first birthday. Besides warm winter clothes, most of them hand-me-downs from Jutta's little boy, she received a set of wooden blocks that depicted different scenes from fairytales, and several other little toys from neighbors and playmates.

With money from cigarettes I had squirreled away, I bought a few presents for my parents—toilet soap, shaving soap, and a new oilcloth for the table—items still considered luxuries. For Robert I bartered a beer stein as a souvenir from Munich. But I was desperate to find shoes for Luzi. She had outgrown the white leather lace-up booties my mother had saved from when I was a baby.

We all eagerly awaited Luzi's reaction on Christmas Eve, when the tree was lit and we showed her what *Christkindl* (Christ child) had put under it for her. She could have cared less about the clothes, showed only little interest in the rag doll my mother and I had made for her, but was fascinated by the tree's glittery ornaments, and especially by the candlelight. Already fast on her feet, she would have brought the tree down had we let her out of our sight.

Robert's time in Germany was running out. Finally, by the end of January 1949, the paperwork came through. We had permission to marry. I spent sleepless nights debating within myself if marrying Robert and following him to America was the right decision. One part of me shouted, "Don't marry him! He is no good." Another part urged me to break out of my present situation where I saw no future for my child or for myself. The unknown, no matter how dim, held more promise than what I saw ahead if I stayed.

Sometimes, I fantasized that Pepi had miraculously survived and came back. All my troubles would be over. To him, I could have explained the events that brought me to the present situation. He would have understood and rescued Luzi and me, and we would have built a happy life together. But that was fantasy. Reality promised, that unless I married Robert and followed him to the United States, I would be stuck for years, decades maybe, to live under the same roof with my parents, in constant discord with my mother, and my child and I would be branded as the unwed mother of an Ami baby. As my career as a dancer withered away, what would I do? How would I earn a living in post-war Germany? Would my child's future be a repeat of my father's past?

If you work hard, you can become a good maid someday.

These words haunted me like a dark prophecy. I could already feel the social chains tightening, pulling me down, holding me prisoner of birth and circumstance. Weighing all the odds, I opted for the unknown. I had to marry Robert.

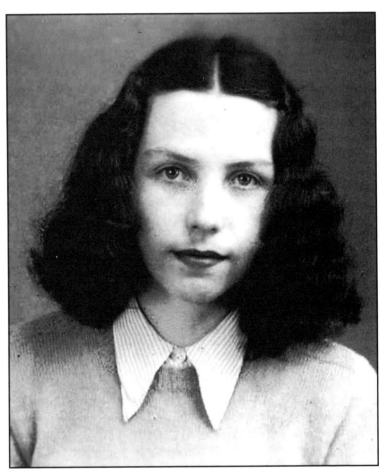

Mitzi, 1949.

Wedding.

On our way to the airport.

Leaving Munich.

American Aunt Mathie.

Chapter 17

The Wedding

January and February dragged on cold and gray. New snow occasionally covered the dirty residue of the old, temporarily lifting the gloom. Shawled women trudged phantom-like through the fog and mist to do their daily shopping. Hardly a sound broke the depressing silence in the residential streets. In pre-war times, these were the months Munich pulsated with merriment. This was *Fasching* (Mardi gras) time, and no matter how gloomy the sky, or how ugly the weather, gaily colored confetti and serpentines danced in the wind; laughter and animated voices rose out of the fog.

So many wonderful, exciting traditions and celebrations had brightened life in pre-war Germany even for the poorest, even during Hitler times. Many were church related or left over from pagan times. The war had taken it all. I felt robbed: robbed of my childhood, robbed of my brother, sweetheart, and friends. Robbed of most of what I loved and enjoyed about my homeland. Detached, anchorless, swept along by the torrents of the time, I found pause and purpose only when I looked into the sweet face and innocent eyes of my child. When her little hands reached out to me and she called, "Mommy," and she hugged me tight, that alone kept me going.

I was planning my wedding. It had to be a wedding due to pressure from all sides. My neighbors, Frau Kloh and Frau Pinzack, volunteered to set up and cater a small reception at my house after the ceremonies. I had to decide what Luzi and I would wear, and what flowers to order. Luzi was going to be my little flower girl. I crocheted her a pale pink-and-white dress and a band with pink flowers for her hair. For myself, I envisioned a long black dress and a bouquet of calla lilies.

"My God, this is your wedding, not your funeral," Frau Pinzack and everyone else protested when they heard of my plans.

I had to laugh. A black dress had just seemed more practical, easier to find, and certainly more appropriate than a white dress. After all, I was not a virgin anymore. On second thought, however, it could have been one of those subconscious, Freudian slips. I was feeling more like preparing for a funeral, than for a wedding.

Munich still did not have a dress shop or department store. All business was conducted out of holes in the wall or temporary stands, or out of somebody's home. Clothing was limited to maybe a short rack of look-alike winter coats, aprons, and scarves, and they were sold out in minutes. With yard goods, it was the same. I finally located a rental place for wedding dresses. They had only white dresses, and among them only one that fit me—a simple, floor-length satin number that came with a veil and a white fur cape. Time was running short. Robert urged me to take it.

218

It was not easy, but little by little, with the help from neighbors, Major Giagandit and his staff, everything came together. Major Giagandit supplied transportation for the wedding party and invited everyone to the radio station for drinks in the evening after the wedding.

On the eve before, Mama pulled a small, metal box from the bottom of her wardrobe where she had kept important papers and a few pieces of jewelry from her mother, including a treasured diamond ring.

"I can't stop you from marrying Robert, but I want to give you something, an insurance policy, so if things don't work out, you can buy a ticket home."

She took out a small, red velvet etui, opened it and stared at it, dumbstruck. It was empty. "Where is the ring? It's gone!" She dumped the contents of the box out on her bed, but there was no ring. She turned to me. "Did you take it out for some reason?"

"Of course not. I don't get into your stuff."

"Maybe Papa took it out. He always wanted to get it appraised."

Papa was not home at the time. Mama paced the floor, pulling her hair, trying to remember if perhaps she had taken the ring out, put it down some place and forgot. Finally, Papa came home. They started searching the entire apartment.

Mama suddenly stopped. "Robert!" The name popped out of her mouth like the cork from a bottle, releasing the evil spirits within to play havoc with our destiny.

"He was present when I brought out the box and looked for your birth certificate," she said.

We stood in disbelief and shock. Even Mama, who had never liked or trusted Robert, had trouble suspecting him of stealing an heirloom from us. All I could think of was, "Oh, my God! What shall I do? Tomorrow morning is the wedding."

It seemed as if all the blood had drained from my body. "What if it is true that Robert stole the ring? What if I accuse him of it, cancel the wedding then find out that he is innocent?"

My parents and I stayed up long past midnight, debating how to proceed. When we finally trudged off to bed, I stopped at Luzi's crib, sank down to my knees and wept.

None of us got much sleep that night. Early the next morning, neighbors arrived with dishes and chairs. Robert had hired a horse-drawn wedding carriage to take us to the *Standesamt* (registrar). We had to be dressed and ready by nine o'clock.

Smile, even if your heart is breaking!

On the Russian front, I had gotten lots of practice to turn off my feelings, smiling and dancing for the wounded and dying, when my heart was breaking, or when I felt death breathing down on me. Then as now, I carried on, going through the motions. *The show must go on!*

At first, my parents said that they would not attend the wedding. Though they had no proof, they concluded that only Robert could have taken the ring. Finally, they, too, capitulated to social pressure.

It was a gray, rainy day. Someone said that rain on a wedding day was a sign of good luck. The carriage arrived punctually, followed by Robert and a fellow from the station with a car.

"Hello Darling," Robert greeted me, all smiles, trying to pull me into his arms. Instinctively, I shrank back from him, unable to even look him in the face.

"Is anything the matter?" he asked, surveying the gloom on my and my parents' faces.

220

"It's just wedding jitters," Frau Pinzack, who over-heard his question, explained with a chuckle.

The fellow who came with Robert brought in the bouquet—calla lilies. Now I wished I had stuck with a black dress. It really felt like going to my funeral.

Robert and I rode in the carriage. Mama and Papa rode in the car. At the registrar's office, we met our witnesses: Adele and her son, and a couple of Robert's buddies. Our party filled the small, dreary office of the registrar, where already two other couples waited to sign their papers. Bomb damage was still visible everywhere, from broken and patched windows, to exposed bricks where mortar had fallen off the walls. The registrar, a balding, round-faced older man, leafed stone-faced through huge ledgers, called the next couple in line to the counter and shoved some papers under their nose. He had on woolen gloves from which the fingertips were cut away. I watched as the party in front of ours dipped the pen into an inkwell and, one by one, scratched their signatures on the documents. The registrar quickly blotted the ink between each sign-ing, and when they were done, looked up and, with-out even looking at the newly-weds said, "You are now legally married."

"Couldn't he have at least looked up and smiled? Damn bureaucrats," I thought.

From the registrar, our party drove to a chapel, lo-cated in the former Nazi warehouse from which I had stolen the Nazi flag. It was now an American military headquarters. Awaiting us was an army chaplain and several neighbors with Luzi, who proudly carried her flower basket and was not about to let go of it.

The chapel was plain, but bright and cheery, and the chaplain greeted everybody with a warm, friendly smile. What a difference, after the stiff, solemn, cold atmosphere at the registrar's office. It greatly elevated everyone's mood. Even I felt suddenly more optimistic again. Now I was glad that Robert had insisted on also having a church wedding.

While the chaplain instructed all wedding participants in the sequence of the ceremony, guests seated themselves in the chapel on rows of folding chairs. Robert had chosen a fellow from the radio station to be his best man; I chose my best friend, Hanni, as my maid of honor.

I had never been at a wedding and knew very little about customs, except what I had seen in movies. So, I simply followed along and did what I was told.

Outside, the rain clouds had parted. A shaft of sunlight flooded the raised altar. On one side of it stood a lectern, and beside it an American flag; on the other side stood a small organ where a young Ami soldier sat playing hymns. When everything seemed to be in place, the chaplain stepped in front of the altar, nodded to the organist, who paused, then signaled us in the back of the chapel to start walking down the aisle. The organist started up again. I recognized the melody. It was the wedding march from Wagner's opera *Lohengren*. "Strange. Hadn't Wagner's music been banned in Germany?" The weirdest thoughts blitzed through my mind as I walked down that aisle, totally unrelated to the present. I was so nervous that nothing made sense anymore.

Luzi had been cranky. She wanted to be with Oma and Opa. One of her older playmates was supposed to walk with her, but Luzi slipped out of her grip and ran as fast as her little legs could go, down that aisle and into my father's arms. She stole the show.

I had some problems understanding and repeating the wedding vows, stumbling over unfamiliar words. Otherwise, the ceremony proceeded and concluded flawlessly. I held together, rigid, as if stuck inside a steel armor. When it was over, the steel melted. I was near collapse.

On the way out of the chapel, Robert's buddies congratulated and threw rice at us. At home, everything was ready. Our neighbors had cleared out my room to set up an L-shaped table, covered with white bed sheets and decorated with little snowbells—the first flowers of spring. After a dinner of roasts and dumplings, they carried in a big, rectangular cake with white frosting, filled glasses with champagne and toasted our married future. Even old, asthmatic Herr Kloh joined us, and presented me with one of his watercolors. All the gifts were small personal items—an ink drawing of Munich, a poem, a book, a vase, a lace doily. I treasured them. They were the best people had to give.

In the company of our merry guests, my parents and I forgot about the ring for a few hours. Even after most had left, the rest of us had to quickly pitch in to clean up, return borrowed items, and get ready for the party at the radio station.

The first floor of the *Kaulbach Villa* featured a huge room, furnished with several comfortable couches and chairs, leaving plenty of space to fill in with straight-back or folding chairs to accommodate a large gathering. Its focal point was an enormous chandelier hanging in the center. Another, smaller one hung inside a generous alcove under the stairs, a kind of study or library.

The party was already well primed when Robert and I arrived. Major Giagandit greeted us with a few congratulatory words and directed us to the bar to get a drink. It had everything from beer to champagne. The preferred drink that night was *arrak*, comparable to ouzo. Before the war, my mother had used it, along with rum, to flavor her Christmas Stollen. I had not seen any since.

After a few short speeches and toasts, honoring our wedding day, fellows cleared a small area and invited us to dance to music piped in from the broadcasting room. Some of the men had brought their girlfriends.

Soon, the *arrak* took effect. One after another, fellows wandered off, some passed out, and a few took center stage with acrobatic antics. One in particular insisted he had wings and could fly. He climbed up the stairs and over the railing, and then slid down the wire of the chandelier and was swinging on it like a monkey. The fellow, Albert Salmi, survived to later become a well-known character actor in Hollywood.

Robert hung out in the bathroom, bellowing like a seal, loud enough that everyone could hear him. A buddy of his, who was still halfway sober, took me home. Robert went to sickbay, and I was spared the dreaded wedding night.

Major Giagandit had arranged for Robert and me to spend a short honeymoon at the Eibsee, an alpine resort, where he assigned Robert to cover a winter sports event. We had to leave the next morning. Robert showed up at my house with a hangover 'a la grande' which lasted for several days, inhibiting his amorous intentions. He needed aspirin more than he wanted me.

My parents, in the meantime, had reported the theft of the ring to the German police, who took fingerprints off the box. They found one print that did not match ours. Next time Robert was at our house, Papa handed him a carefully polished glass to drink from and later turned it over to the detective handling the case.

"Oh, God, let it not be a match," I prayed. With all my heart, I wanted to find Robert innocent and begin married life, devoted to the sanctity of its meaning and purpose.

Chapter 18

Show Down

𝕽obert and I had been married for less than a week, with just days left before he had to leave Germany. The paperwork for my visa and for the transport of our household goods had still not come through. It worried me less than the still unresolved matter of the stolen ring. Tension at home burned an ulcer into my stomach. When my mother was not ranting, deep, bitter lines drew down the corners of her mouth. My father, who was better at hiding his feelings, developed a tremor in his hands as soon as Robert appeared on the scene.

My worst fears had come true. The fingerprints on the glass matched the print on the case that had held my mother's ring.

"Act normal," the detective instructed us. "Don't let on that you are missing the ring and that you suspect Robert. I need the element of surprise to nail this case, and solid evidence to gain the cooperation of American authorities."

225

"What more proof do you need?"

"Give me a few more days. The matching finger-prints are still no proof that he stole the ring," the detective cautioned us.

"A few more days?" my mother postured. "He'll be gone, so will be the ring, and that'll be it."

A tense silence hung over us, like the charged silence before a breaking storm. To act as if nothing had happened became unbearable. Robert must have sensed that something was up.

The day after the detective gave us the result of the fingerprints, Major Giagandit summoned my parents and me to the radio station for a meeting, regarding a police investigation. We complied, nerves frayed, not knowing what to expect.

We found the Major in his office, sitting behind a desk stacked high with files and papers. Though the door was open, we knocked before entering.

"Thank you for coming," the Major greeted us. He rose from his chair, shut the door behind us and invited us to sit down. Back at his desk again, he opened a drawer, took out a folded envelope, opened it and took out a ring. Holding it up he asked, "Is this your ring?" It was.

Responding to our baffled stares, he explained. "A detective from the German police was here yesterday. He informed me of the situation and asked permission to interview my staff, especially Robert's roommates. In my presence, some of them testified that Robert had approached them, trying to sell a diamond ring. I called Robert into my office. My first concern was, if possible, to get you your ring back." He handed the ring to my mother, who took it, temporarily lost for words.

The Major leaned back in his chair and relit his ever-present pipe. "At first, Robert denied everything," he continued, "but in the face of overwhelming evidence, he confessed. I could have had him arrested right then, but I was thinking of his young wife and child." Pausing, his eyes switched back and forth between my parents and me, trying to read our feelings. I broke down crying.

"I told my daughter, he is no good. He belongs in jail," my mother blurted out.

Ignoring her outburst, the Major went on. "Robert seems to be genuinely sorry, claiming that he was distraught because he had no money to leave his wife and child."

"Pffff..." my mother exploded again. "He is a thief...a common thief."

Major Giagandit straightened in his chair. "I'll leave it up to you to press charges." Keeping his eyes fixed on my mother, he said, "Before you decide, do consider this: Robert comes from a good, well respected, well-to-do family in the United States. Young soldiers over here sometimes think they can get away with things they would never dream of doing back home. If you press charges, it will be on his record forever. He will have a hard time finding a decent job, thus be unable to support his wife and child. And if he goes to jail now, chances are, you'll never see or hear from him again. His child will never know her father. His marriage may even be annulled." He paused to let his words sink in. "My advice is to give him another chance."

The Major stood up. "I will leave you alone for awhile to think this over."

Heading out the door, he stopped short to give me a sympathetic pat on the shoulder.

I translated for my father what the Major had said, but my mother's ranting made it difficult. "Sorry...he is sorry? Hah," she mocked. Having to vent her anger, she turned on me, "You should have listened to me, but you never do. I don't count. You could have had your pick from dozens of nice guys. I don't understand what you see in him."

Finally, unable to hold my tongue any longer, I lashed back. "If I could just talk to you, I wouldn't be in this fix."

"Ahh...so now it's my fault?"

"Stop it," my father cut in. "This is not the time or place to argue." Looking at my mother, he repeated, "Stop it! We have to decide what to do." I had never heard him use such a harsh tone with her.

In a way, it would have been simple justice to let Robert pay for his crime. Justice, however, I was beginning to learn, was seldom that simple. The innocent often paid with the guilty. In this case, he would go to prison, but so would I...in a different sort of way. My child and I would be sentenced to live in the bleak, depressing circumstances, under the same roof with my parents for years to come, hostage to my mother's constant nagging, cast aside by a judgmental society. What would I do? How would I provide for us?

Though I neither loved nor respected Robert, at the time, he was my only hope to break out of my present chains. Fair or not, after what he did to me, I had no trouble to quiet my conscience.

Mama already had her mind set to press charges. My father let her rant on, saying very little. I tuned her out, giving way to bitter, long harbored resentments from childhood. It seemed, I could never meet my mother's ambitions, or fill my father's lack of them.

Up boiled the unfulfilled longings of a child denied to run, laugh and play like other children; the hurt of ridicule for being made to stand out with corkscrew curls and frou-frou dresses from American cousins; the humiliation for having to pass a plate like a beggar after dancing in outdoor cafes during summer months.

I resented the load no child should have to carry. If I stayed home, the burden of expectation would ride me into the ground.

In normal times, I could have moved out and on, and would not be in this situation in the first place. But these were not normal times. I wanted out.

I looked at Papa. "I want to work it out with Robert. He is Luzi's father. I can't stay here...I can't stay," I sobbed.

"That criminal! He means more to her than we do." My mother threw up her hands.

The Major returned. "Well? Have you decided?"

"If Robert is here, I would like to talk to him, alone. He understands enough German to get my point," my father said to him. "It'll take just a few minutes." I translated for the Major.

"Very well, I'll call him."

Mama and I retreated to the foyer, pacing the floor. Mama did not speak to me.

After about ten minutes, Papa came out. "If you want to say goodbye to him, this is your last chance," he said to me. Reluctantly, I went back to the office to face Robert. He was awash with tears and fell to his knees, grabbing my hand. "Please, please forgive me. I will do my best to be a good husband and father. I'll prove to you that I can change. I love you. Please give me another chance. Everything will be different from now on."

"For the sake of our child, I'll try," I said, pulling my hand out of his. "Just know, I don't love you, and I can't ever love you until I can respect you."

Not only did I not love him, I despised him for what he did, but at that moment, deep in my heart stirred pity for him. I wanted to believe that he would change and that he, Luzi and I could become a family. In case things did not work out, I had aunts in America who would help me.

Before my parents and I left the radio station, the Major took me aside. "If you have any more problems down the line, don't hesitate to contact me. I put a sealed envelope with the police report in Robert's file. Should he mess up, it will be opened and he will be prosecuted. For now, I wish you and your child the best of luck." We shook hands. "You will like it in America."

It was a relief that Robert was gone. But even without him, life at home was no picnic. Every day confirmed that I had made the right decision to leave. My friends Jutta and Hanni could not believe that I was really leaving my homeland.

"I could never do that," Hanni said and shook her head. "I would die from homesickness."

"So would I," Jutta agreed.

When I looked at the bigger picture, I realized that my parents wanted and did the best they could for me. I did not understand then, but already suspected that painful experiences of their own dictated their actions and behavior. I would miss them. So would little Luzi. She was the sunshine in our lives. My parents doted on her.

I would also miss the Bavarian landscape with its snow-covered peaks. From what Robert had told me, Nebraska, the state he called home, had no mountains, no forests, only cornfields as far as the eye can see. I had a hard time imagining not being able to escape into the cool silence of a forest, or seeing the white, jagged outline of the Alps in the distance. He had told me about cattle ranches and cowboys, about fireflies and the song of crickets at night, and about elm trees turning golden in fall. It all sounded very interesting, but it was hard to give up the last symbol of permanence and of home, that piece of earth where I grew up and where my soul was rooted.

After Robert had left Germany, I had to have several more VD tests, one of the most degrading experiences in my life. Finally, the immigration office notified me to come in for an interview. My interviewer was a middle-aged man, an American in civilian clothes and not the friendliest guy. He asked me what I knew about America and Nebraska. I told him what Robert had told me. "Add tornados, 100 degree temperatures in the summer, and paralyzing blizzards in the winter," he sneered. Leafing through my records, he said, "I see you are a dancer. What kind of dancer?"

"I was trained in ballet and interpretive dance."

"Where did you dance?" He went on to ask the same stupid questions in the same sarcastic tone as the interviewer at Geiselgasteig, when I applied for a job in the film industry.

"You danced for the Nazis? Did you dance for Hitler?"

He saw a conflict in my dancing for *Nazi* soldiers, as he called them, when I claimed never having been a member of the Nazi party. I reckoned that the interview would have gone a lot smoother had I said that I or, at least, my folks were party members. I had to hold my tongue, but his attitude concerned me. It was based on the assumption that all Germans had to have been Nazis, and I wondered how widely spread this was.

In the meantime, I had received several letters from Robert in which he described his happiness to set foot on American soil again, and how he and a few buddies got drunk, celebrating their landing in New York. "The first thing I ordered was a tall glass of fresh cold milk, and a big steak," he wrote. Back in Nebraska, his father had arranged a job interview for him at a prestigious hotel where he hired on as a desk clerk with potential to advance to a manager's position.

In all of his letters, he professed his love and devotion to Luzi and me, but mentioned nothing about the airline ticket. He had wanted me to fly to America rather than travel by ship, planning to use his discharge bonus to pay for it. I was biting my fingernails as the days moved closer and closer to the deadline when the movers were scheduled to come to pack and ship off my belongings to the United States. What if he never sends me that ticket? Mama walked around with a smug expression that said, "I told you so. He is no good." She was hoping, of course, that I would never get that ticket. Then, just in the nick of time, I received a telegram from Robert that I could pick up the ticket at the airport.

Now it was the middle of May. The movers came to pack up the household goods, consisting of bedding, dishes, and odds and ends Robert had purchased, plus my piano. When Mama heard that I wanted to take the piano, she exploded. "The piano stays here," she insisted.

"Why? It is my piano. I worked and paid for it," I told her.

"The piano does not leave this house," Mama told the packers, who looked confused from one to the other.

This was the last straw. It confirmed that if I stayed I would never own anything, including my life.

The fight over my piano turned embarrassingly ugly. My father finally intervened by leading Mama out of my room into the kitchen, nodding to the packers to go ahead with their job. This incident widened the split between my mother and me even further. For my mother, the piano was, perhaps, the last desperate hold she had on me. For me, it was my only and most precious possession.

At that time, I could not understand my mother's motives. Neither of my parents played the piano, and as soon as I had moved out, someone else would be moving in. Living space was still so scarce that the housing authorities had to exercise control over every square inch. My room with everything in it would be assigned to somebody, anybody, giving preference to Nazi victims first, and the most desperate cases next, not exempting bribery. My parents had little choice in the matter. For somebody else, my piano would only take up precious space.

I doubt if my mother ever analyzed her actions or reactions, or understood the motives that drove them. Even many years later, to the very end of her long life, it was impossible to engage in a rational dialogue with her. We were two souls on opposite sides of a river that ran swift and deep, and neither one of us knew how to bridge it.

The packers had finished, their truck was loaded, and they left. My room looked empty without the piano, empty like my heart. In a few more days, Luzi and I would be gone also. Then fate took another twist. I received a letter from the movie set in Geiselgasteig that I was being considered for a role in a circus film. A friend had recommended me for it. Was this the break I had been waiting for? I hid the letter, wanting time to think about it. If Mama found out about this, it would just cause another blow-up.

Without my parent's knowing, I looked up my friend, the playwright, to find out more about this. Yes, he said, I had an excellent chance to land the part, but it would be six months before the actual shooting of the movie began.

"Six months," I pondered, "and it's not a 100% sure thing?"

"This is your big chance," my friend encouraged me.

It was tempting. But I would forfeit my visa, forfeit my ticket, lose my piano, and in the meantime be stuck at home without a job or income. And if the deal should fall through...? The prospects of that were more than I could handle.

I left my friend, saying that I would think it over. By the time I was back home, I had already made up my mind. I could not do it.

Chapter 19

Goodbyes

$\mathfrak{J}$n 1949, air travel over the oceans was not only considered a risky adventure, it was expensive as well. When I went to the airport to pick up my ticket and watched a two-engine plane take off, my heart skipped a couple of beats. I was both excited and scared. Over the next days, I scanned newspapers and listened to the radio for reports on any recent plane crashes. There were none. I became a little more confident.

Frau Klara had tailored a chic travel suit for me made from a pinstriped, gray wool cloth. With money received as a wedding present from Robert's associates at the radio station, I purchased a red blouse, red, platform sandals made of wood, (my first pair of new shoes since 1943) and a red purse to go with the suit. Luzi had grown into the blue pinafore dress her American grandparents had sent, and I crocheted her a lacy skirt and blouse. I thought this would do her for the trip. She was almost potty-trained, but on the plane, I knew

I had to rely on diapers and fretted that I would not have enough.

The day for my departure was set for June 8. I would be taking a two-engine plane from Munich to Brussels, where I had to transfer to a four-engine DC6 to cross the ocean—destination New York. After a short stay with my aunts, who had promised to pick Luzi and me up from the airport, I would be taking another plane to Omaha, Nebraska, where Robert was waiting for me.

The last weeks and days before leaving my parents and my homeland, I spent visiting and saying goodbye to many of my friends, some against my mother's wishes, since she had had a falling out with them. I wanted very much to see my eight-grade teacher again and thank her one more time for the many hours she had spent tutoring me for the entrance exam to the university. She had given me confidence that I had a mind as good as anybody else's. I went to her last known address in downtown Munich, but the house was gone. The whole area looked like a giant quarry. As I stood there, wondering if she had survived, I could still see her, riding to school on her motorbike, which was quite uncommon for a woman at the time. She did not seem to care what people thought. And in class, she was often quite outspoken when she disagreed with something in the curriculum, treading danger-ously close to the political edge. She was strong and she had guts. Remembering her, I caught myself smiling while tears rolled down my face. I would never see her again.

Another important person in my life was my dance teacher Lisa Kresse. Bombed out in Munich, she had found shelter in a garage in a suburb of Munich. My parents and I visited her and marveled how she had turned an unfinished shed into a bright and inviting place to live by using odds and ends, cardboards, and a paintbrush. All it lacked was a stove, and during the first winter, a neighbor found her unconscious and almost frozen to death.

Lisa Kresse was an artist through and through, who liberated me from the rigidity of ballet, teaching me that dance was more than turning pirouettes. Once celebrated world wide, she plummeted into oblivion—first, because of a drug addiction, later because she had married a Jew, a world famous violinist. Recovering from her addiction, hard and horrible as it was, proved easier than overcoming Nazi discrimination. She remained blacklisted, though she had already been divorced and remarried an Arian.

I was six years old when I became her protégée, and worked with and under her until I joined the Molkow Ballet in Berlin at the age of fifteen. Lisa Kresse's life was a string of tragedies and ended in a drug and alcohol induced stupor sometime in the late fifties.

The goodbyes were many, heart wrenching and tearful, but none was as hard as saying goodbye to my parents. For days already, my mother could not stop crying. "I'll never see you or Luzi again. You are all I have, my only child." Every so often, I saw Papa wiping his eyes, also. I cried into my pillow at night, my heart in a merciless squeeze between past and future. Little Luzi was happy and oblivious to it all. Her heartache would come later, when she would call for Oma and Opa and I had to explain why they are not there.

My suitcases were packed and tagged, a large one and a smaller one, plus a large satchel with Luzi's blanket, diapers, bottles, formula, and a change of clothes. The day and hour of departure was here. I took one more look around: at my room with the blue furniture; the kitchen with its rickety buffet and upholstered bench with an assortment of handcrafted pillows

Mama and I had made; the back yard with the clotheslines and beyond the greenbelt with its filled-in but still
visible bomb craters.

Our dog, Baerli, did not leave Luzi's side. When he
saw us putting on jackets and coats, he slinked, tail
between his legs, into my room and under Luzi's crib.
I think he sensed that he would not see his playmate
again.

Before leaving the house, I double-checked that I
had all the necessary papers, the ticket, ID, and visa in
my purse. Papa carried the big suitcase; I carried the
rest. Mama held on to Luzi.

Papa had already locked the door behind him when
our neighbor, old Herr Kloh called out of his window.
"Mitzi, wait...wait... I want to give you something." It
was a small, silver St. Christopher medal. "Keep it with
you and you'll be safe," he said, struggling for breath.
I thanked him. Good old Kloh, I thought, this may be
the last time I see him. He was so sick. On the way to
the tram stop, neighbors waved and wished me a safe
journey.

It had been raining on and off. Though it was June,
it was unseasonably cool, and I wished I had left my
coat unpacked. On the long ride to the airport, we
had to transfer twice, then take a bus for the last stretch
to the terminal. We talked very little on the way. My
throat was choked with the memories of twenty-three
years, a color palette of emotions. My parents may have
felt the same. Papa stopped now and then to take a
picture of us with his box camera.

Once inside the terminal, we checked my large suitcase, which I would not see again until I went through
customs in New York. We had an hour before my flight
would leave. These were the most agonizing, heart-
wrenching minutes in my life. I kept assuring my parents that I would come back to visit. "It only takes a

day and night to get here," I said, though I knew that it would be more complicated than that.

Only Luzi's fussing and crying—she was hungry and sleepy by now—temporarily diverted our attention away from our pain. Cradling her on my lap, I started to tell her a story about a magic bird that would carry us up, up to the clouds, and faraway to an enchanted land. We would live in a house with a huge garden, full of flowers and butterflies, and a big tree with a swing. At night she could watch the fireflies with their little lanterns that twinkled like the stars. And she could look up at the moon, that big *Balli* in the sky...and... Luzi had fallen asleep, sucking her thumb.

Finally, a plane taxied up to the tarmac and a loud-speaker called passengers to start boarding. Shaking with sobs, we exchanged one more kiss, one more hug, and with Luzi in my arms, I walked away—away from the past and toward the future.

The plane was full. From my window seat I saw my parents standing among several other people, hand-kerchiefs in hand, alternately waving and drying their tears with it. I waved back, wondering if they could see us through the grazed window. Then, with a roar, the propellers started up, the plane vibrated and started to move, slow at first, taxiing into position for take-off, then faster and faster, its wheels chattering over the rough runway. Suddenly I felt a lift. We were in the air. As we gained altitude, my parents and the terminal kept shrinking away. People on the ground became unrecognizable dots. Below us lay Munich. Reaching up from her ruins, I vaguely recognized a few remaining landmarks—the spire of St. Peter's church and the round steeples of the *Frauenkirche*. I caught a brief glimpse of snow-covered peaks and patches of forest before we ascended into the clouds.

"Goodbye, Munich. Goodbye mountains and woods and land that I love."

As my heart drummed out these last goodbyes to my homeland, I sensed that part of me would forever stay there, and part of it would always be with me.

Epilogue

As the plane soared higher and higher, it broke through the clouds into a bright, clear-blue sky. The emotional weight of the last hours, days, months and years seemed to float away from me like the cotton puffs outside the plane's window. My heart felt suddenly light and free, like being lifted out of bondage. My mind focused trained on tomorrow, allowing youthful dreams to reemerge. I rediscovered my strength of will. Stroking the golden locks of my sleeping child, I silently vowed, "What ever it takes, we will make it."

The landing in Brussels was bumpy and hard. So was the sobering reality I faced.

Uniformed airport personnel checked the tickets and visas of all disembarking passengers, allowing some to enter Belgium, while others, traveling on to New York, had to stay and spend the night in barracks within a fenced-off area next to the airport. An attendant with a clipboard read off names from the latter group and led them to their quarters. Another young war bride, Luzi and I were left standing in the rain, and told to wait. We quickly sought shelter under the eaves of the nearest barracks. Besides carrying Luzi, I had to tote two big bags, almost dropping under the weight.

After about ten minutes or more, the attendant, a uniformed female returned and asked us in English to follow her. She saw me struggle with my bags but lent no hand.

She showed us to a room in one of the buildings where six narrow cots, a small table and chair lined the walls. It was cold, stark, but clean. Before leaving, the attendant pointed to an adjacent building. "Over there is the cafeteria. Dinner is at six." With that, she left.

Luzi had been cranky. She was hungry, thirsty, and had dirtied her diaper. I changed her, then got water from a sink at the end of a long hallway, added a little powdered milk and gave it to her. The airline had assured me that I would find special provisions for my child along the way. So far, I was on my own.

At six, my roommate, Luzi, and I went to the cafeteria. Other passengers from our flight were sitting in the dining room, already eating. We sought to join them.

"The dining room is closed," a waiter stopped us, und directed us to an area off the kitchen where waiters placed and picked up their orders, and where employees took their breaks.

"You may sit here."

My roommate and I exchanged baffled glances, but neither of us said anything. We sat down at a bare table and waited. I had my hands full entertaining Luzi, who wanted to explore her new surroundings.

Finally, the waiter—a Frenchman, judging by his accent—set the table and brought two bowls of soup. I wondered why he did not show us a menu. After the soup, which I shared with Luzi, we were served steak with spinach and potatoes. It looked good, and we were hungry.

"Excuse me, could you bring..." The waiter had slid the plates in front of us and disappeared before I could finish asking for an extra plate and glass of milk for my child. His brusque manner was intimidating, as if he was doing us a great favor by waiting on us.

My roommate was about to take her first bite when she rumpled her nose and said, "Something smells awful. It's the meat." She laid down her fork, almost gagging.

242

I had noticed it, too. "It *is* the meat. It smells rotten," I agreed.

We called the waiter and complained.

"What do you mean? This is perfectly good steak. It's just well aged," he said.

"Smell it. It is bad," I countered.

"Well," the waiter blustered, "if you don't like it, leave it."

"Can you bring us something else instead, please?"

"The cook has left. The kitchen is closed," he said and walked off.

"Just one minute," I called after him. "We have not had anything to eat all day. Neither has my child. I must insist that you bring us something, at least some milk and sandwiches."

"I am no cook. The day for you Germans to make demands is over," the waiter replied without looking back.

We sat there, not knowing what to do. Since there was no one around, and we were still so hungry, we finally ate the spinach and potatoes, and returned to our room.

◆ ◆ ◆

This little episode made me wonder and fear what I could expect ahead. As I soon found out, the shadow of my national past followed me to the 'land of the free', and the 'sorting out' my GI friend Morris Katz had promised, never happened publicly; it was left to the individual.

On to America!

**Order Form for
autographed copies**

Please ship _____ **copies of** $\mathfrak{Shadow\ of\ Defeat}$

Please ship _____ **copies of** $\mathfrak{Dancing\ to\ War}$

TO:

Name: _____

Address: _____

State: _____   Zip: _____

Retail Price: $16.95 each
Please include $3.00 per copy for shipping

Send check to:
Elfi Hornby
PO Box 25477
Federal Way, WA 98093-2377